Hey, I'm Marty. I Drive the Bus

If You Have Ever Driven A Bus Or Have Been A Passenger On A Bus, You Must Read This Book

by
Marty Molinaro

authorHOUSE®

AuthorHouse™
1663 Liberty Drive, Suite 200
Bloomington, IN 47403
www.authorhouse.com
Phone: 1-800-839-8640

© 2008 Marty Molinaro. All rights reserved.

No part of this book may be reproduced, stored in a retrieval system, or transmitted by any means without the written permission of the author.

First published by AuthorHouse 10/17/2008

ISBN: 978-1-4389-1136-6 (sc)

Printed in the United States of America
Bloomington, Indiana

This book is printed on acid-free paper.

DEDICATION

To the women in my life

Mom. The woman who raised me and tried to steer me in always making the right choices in life. No matter what I did; she was always there for me. I miss you Mom.

Daughter Wendy, whom I spoiled rotten and always knew that she herself would one day, be a great mom. I can't thank her enough for blessing us with AJ and Alex.

Finally to my wife and best friend, Rose. She is my every breath and the reason that I exist.

Loving Thanks to each of you, for without any of you; my life would have been boring and uneventful. Thanks!!

TABLE OF CONTENTS

Chapter 1	The red sports car	9
Chapter 2	Hey look there's a turtle	13
Chapter 3	The Dolphin Trainer	18
Chapter 4	The Barf-A-Rama	21
Chapter 5	Can you take me to Alabama?	27
Chapter 6	Breast feeding on the bus	32
Chapter 7	Lady please keep your clothes on!!	37
Chapter 8	Large scary guy and the dollar bill	42
Chapter 9	Twenty dollar bill in Traffic	49
Chapter 10	My home is in heaven	56
Chapter 11	The clay fight!	64
Chapter 12	There are no rats and it doesn't stink	72
Chapter 13	You're a penny Shy. I won't move the bus!!	77
Chapter 14	My baby ate the bus transfer!!	88
Chapter 15	So you kids want to play, huh!!	92
Chapter 16	Appling make-up on a moving bus!!	97
Chapter 17	It's OK I don't have germs!!	101

Chapter 18	Cell phones, Doctors and the bus!!	105
Chapter 19	Frustrated woman and her Psychiatrist!!	109
Chapter 20	Kids are spoiled rotten these days!!	111
Chapter 21	College Girls!!	117
Chapter 22	Young couple fighting on bus!!	120
Chapter 23	To busy listening to his radio!!	125
Chapter 24	Could you drop me off at the Bank?	129
Chapter 25	Animals on the bus!!	137
Chapter 26	Hey, discipline the kid will ya?	143
Chapter 27	Boogers! Breakfast of champions!!	149

INTRODUCTION

My name is Marty and I drive a city transit bus. Bus driving is an occupation that puts you in, up front and personal with a special sector of our society. I have accumulated a variety of anecdotes that I wish to share. Many of these situations are serious while others are mind boggling, hilarious or just make you want to say, "Oh, what were they thinking." Having personally been involved and witnessing these scenarios have made it possible for me to look forward in going to work everyday and hopefully experiencing more. I've included twenty-seven of these short stories because I felt that twenty-eight was just to many too read; and besides I plan on releasing another twenty-seven stories in the future book.

People say and do the most amazing things. Usually preconceived notions and actions before thinking make situations, which normally should have simple outcomes, become more complicated than they actually are. These miscommunications offer memorable stories and anecdotes.

City transits systems are becoming more and more complicated due to the fact more people are riding the bus. Schedules are made per rider-ship volume and peak usage times to try to accommodate the majority of the people. Utilization of the transit equipment and costs are taken into account when schedules are created to minimize equipment and operation costs. The bus riders don't care about any of this. All they worry about is what time the bus comes and what time the bus leaves.

There are numerous reasons why people ride the bus, so let me introduce you to those reasons:

First and foremost there are the individuals that are physically or mentally incapable of operating a private vehicle. This class of individuals has limitations placed on them through no fault of their own. This group typically includes individuals who are physically challenged. I respect these individuals to the utmost for their diligent efforts. Regardless of the weather conditions they man their wheelchairs, walkers or trudge on foot to their assigned buses to reach their appointed destinations. They and the bus driver's typically have special bonds usually it being a love or hate relationship. The bus driver's usually know these bus riders names and the bus riders know the bus driver's names. Many times theses passengers know more about the bus driver's private life than the bus driver's wishes that they knew.

The second group there is are the elderly. This group relies on public transportation for everything. This group is the most appreciative and usually the friendliest to the drivers. There are instances where certain elderly passengers will not ride on the bus if a certain driver is driving that bus route. The elderly passenger, for whatever reason, would rather wait for the next bus than ride with that driver. Who knows why?

This group of passengers knows the telephone number of the transit office by memory mainly because they have dialed it so many times to complain about one thing or another. They rely on the bus drivers to help them whenever possible, and sometimes they want to be treated as if they are the sole purpose that the transit system is in business. Many times they reward the bus driver's with gifts to show there appreciation. I've never taken anything of monetary value. However, I've received half eaten donuts, pieces of over ripened fruit; cupcakes with finger prints imbedded in the frosting and an assortment of other delicacies. The gesture's that are given by this group are truly from the heart.

The third of the categories of individuals that ride the bus are those who have had their driving privilege taken away because of unlawful acts for which they have committed.

This group can be divided into two groups with the first group being those that know that they messed up and are trying to make up for their mistakes. Rehabilitation is defiantly a goal for this group of the rider-ship. This group shows remorse for their mistakes and is trying now to do the right things. Most of the time those passengers that are in this segment of our rider-ship have low paying jobs that they must work long hours at. This group too depends on the local transit system to get them around.

The second of this group are those who blame everybody else for their predicament except themselves. Many in this rider-ship group complain about everything. They treat the bus driver as if he or she were to blame for their situation and treat the drivers as if they were their private chauffeur. Many of the individuals that are in this segment of rider-ship typically smell of alcohol and cigarettes. A lot of times they try to talk the bus driver into giving them a free ride. Many passengers in this group are in dire need of learning how to use soap and water. It seems that personal hygiene is for others and not particularly for them. This group never mentions anything about having a steady job. This group of the passenger rider-ship usually tarnishes the efforts of their counterparts who are truly trying to get on with their lives and make a new start for themselves.

The fourth category of passengers includes students. Regardless if they are in grade school, high school or college they all have one thing in common and that is that they usually know everything. Many of these young adults feel that once they set foot on the bus they can do things there that they can't do at home. Most of the young adults are good most of the time; but, they do have their moments. They swear and use language that would make a drunken sailor blush. Many times their conversations include references of bodily functions or simulated sexual activities to emphasize their point. The rules posted on the bus are for somebody else and not for them to follow. Eating, loud music and horseplay is common within this group. After all these young adults are just kids.

Lastly there is the group of transit passengers that ride the bus for convenience or a cause. This group of bus passengers usually has automobiles, but; would rather not spend the money for the gas. Many in this rider-ship group insist that they are protesting petroleum prices. Most of them would classify themselves not as cheapskates; but rather, pennywise. Those in this group most often keep to themselves; but, if something happens on the bus or at a bus transfer center that they do not like, this group of passengers have no qualms of complaining to the driver. This group of passengers complains constantly about the temperature in the bus. If it summer outside they need the air conditioner on and if its winter; the bus driver had better have the heater on.

Heaven forbid if the bus is a few minutes late. They will have no problem in reminding the bus driver that the bus driver's wages are paid through their hard earned tax dollars. They don't take into account that the bus driver has many unforeseen circumstances that can make them late. Traffic is usually the main culprit when a transit bus is running behind schedule. But to them; that's just an excuse and not a reason to be late.

This group of passengers also reminds the bus driver that they personally know the mayor or someone related to the mayor and will have no problem calling to report any driver issues that might occur. Within this group are College professors, recent retires (A.K.A. baby-boomers) and self proclaimed environmentalists. The last of these groups is a dying breed.

To be fair to the passengers, the bus drivers themselves can also be divided into categories. I can place the drivers into one of three distinct categories. The first category being the driver who follows the transit rules to the letter. This driver would never think of thinking for himself, let alone use some common sense. This is a good approach except when driving transit routes a driver needs to be flexible. For instance, after a major snow storm there are usually large snow banks to deal with all over the city. Many times the bus stops are buried under or filled with snow. The driver in this category, heaven forbid, will drop passengers off in front of, on or in the snow bank rather than using common sense and pulling up ten feet to a shoveled sidewalk or drive way. Their excuse is "I stop at the bus stops like my boss told me to do. DUHH!!!!

The next groups of drivers are those who don't care about anyone but themselves. This group of drivers would be happy if they could drive around all day and not be bothered by picking up passengers. All this group wants to do is punch the time clock in, drive their assigned transit route and not be bothered by anyone. This group's motto is "Get in, Shut up and sit down." They follow transit rules, but: will bend them only if it is to their benefit.

I know a driver in this group who fancies himself as always being on time. Keep in mind that buses run on schedules and their main function is to transport passengers. I know of an incident where this certain driver actually left six passengers waiting at a transfer point because he was running a little behind schedule and wanted to keep his so called reputation in tack. He actually cut his route short by about five blocks and missed a shopping center just so that he could get to the end of the bus line on time so that he could eat a sandwich and drink a cup of coffee like he did everyday.

I know this to be true because I dropped those six passengers off at the transfer point and my route ended up at the same route end point as the other drivers did. I asked him if he got the transfers and he said, "What transfers." I said, "The six people that I dropped off at the plaza and radioed dispatch about. I heard over the radio, dispatch telling you about them." His response was, "Aw,

I left them there. I do that all the time. It makes them appreciate the bus more. Besides, management doesn't care, so why should I."

Lastly there is that group of drivers who actually care about their jobs and try to do the right thing. This group shows a compassion for the rider-ship and will use common sense when needed. Many times this group of drivers will bend the transit rules to accommodate the passengers. Some times those who are in this group try too hard to be accommodating to the passengers and ends up regretting their generosity. I know a driver who, with her husbands blessing, in her well meant generosity invited about twenty indigent transit riders to her home for a Thanksgiving dinner. Needless to say in her exuberance to help her fellowman, she brought a nightmare on her family and herself. Her intentions were good, but; she showed a weakness that many of those she invited took advantage of.

While at her house many of those she had invited brought friends and many of those friends were inebriated. She had items stolen out of her house and some of her guests refused to leave after dinner. The police had to be called because one of the guests picked a fight with her husband. The dinner guest was claiming that her husband wasn't good enough for his transit driving wife and that the dinner guest loved her and wanted to be with her forever. To top the day off the rescue squad had to be summoned because one of her guests had an allergic reaction to a strawberry Jell-O mold that she served at the meal. If I'm not mistaken it took about two years of litigation to solve the matter.

Marty Molinaro

In no special or significant order I will try to relate to you my first hand accounts of a gathering of some of my most memorable experiences. In no way am I trying to humiliate or degrade anybody who may be the subject of these stories. They really did it to themselves and I'm just trying to share. I may leave a participle hanging or my verbs may disagree, but: this is the way I talk and I'm telling the stories, so get over it. I drive numerous routes in the city and county and my experiences are not limited to the rich or poor; young or old or any specific ethnic group, but a gathering of all. Enjoy.

Chapter 1

THE RED SPORTS CAR

On one route, I drive through a medical complex which has a circular driveway. Many times cars are parked in the circle making it impossible for the buses to drive through safely. I typically pickup and drop-off passengers near the posted bus stop by the hospital entrance as I drive through the circle. It would be impossible for me to back the bus up, because of obvious safety reason, if cars are parked and blocking the circle. Many times I've pull into the hospital circle only to get stuck and have to wait until someone moves their vehicle before I can continue my route.

People park in the circle when they are dropping patients off or picking them up even though there are legal posted signs directing them that there is no parking at anytime. The traffic at this particular hospital is usually heavy at certain times of the day.

One day a red sports-car was parked in the middle of the circular drive. I did not see the car until I had pulled into the circular drive. I was stuck in the circular drive because I couldn't go forward and I wouldn't back up. I needed to continue with my route, but; first I needed that red sports-car to move before I could move. I could see a person seated behind the steering wheel of the red sports-car. As I pulled up behind the little red car, I tapped on the bus horn. I was hoping that the driver of the red sports-car would get the hint that I need him to move the car so that I could get the bus through and continue with my route. As I was pulling up behind the red sports-car I notice that on top of the car was an open briefcase that obviously was left there by accident. It was then that I noticed that the driver of the car was a younger man perhaps in his mid twenties.

I again tapped on the bus horn to get the drivers attention. My initial thought was for him to get his briefcase off the roof of his car; but, I still needed him to move his car so that I could get the bus through safely. The young man, who was driving the red sports-car, rolled the driver's window down, stuck his hand and arm out of the window and gave an obscene gesture with his middle finger. I again tapped the bus horn to get his attention to make him aware that his briefcase was on the roof of his car. I guess that this was the just too much for him to handle and the wrong thing for me to do. The driver of the red sports-car, obviously angry because I had honked the bus horn at him for the third time, stuck his head out of the open window of his car and started cursing at me as he accelerated rapidly as he drove through the circle drive to the exit. As he sped away papers that were nestled safely in the briefcase started to blow out and around the circle drive and the hospital parking lot. There was nothing that I could do but watch. I felt that I did my part by trying to be a Good Samaritan. After all, maybe he wanted his precious papers spread all over the parking lot.

I pickup a few passengers and proceeded to exit out of the hospital circle drive, driving over many of the papers that the young man in the red sports-car had left behind. The people that I had just picked-up made a comment about how rude the man in the red car was acting. I thought that it was rather comical when one of the wind blown papers actually was blown onto my windshield and got stuck on my windshield wiper. I drove on. After all he didn't care; why should I.

I pulled out of the circle drive and drove up to the stop light near the hospital entrance. There at the stop light, waiting for the light to change, was the red sports-car with the briefcase still on the roof; but, minus its paper contents. The stop and go light was red as I pulled my bus up along side the red sports car with my driver's window even with his passenger window. I again beeped the bus horn again to get the young man in the sports cars attention. I wanted to tell him about his briefcase on his roof and to maybe save the remaining pen and pencils that were in the now almost empty briefcase. He looked my way at the bus and rolled his passenger window down. He had electric windows and just leaned over after the window was open. I figured that he was going to ask me what I wanted and why I was honking the bus horn at him. Nope, that was not his intentions. He didn't care who I was or what I wanted. He again started yelling and screaming obscenities at me.

I sat there smiling and listening to his verbal assault because I knew that I couldn't get a word in even if I had tried to. I waited patiently until he stops yelling at me. I hope that the traffic light doesn't change to green until I have a chance to say something. The angry young man finally stopped yelling and I had a chance to say what was on my mind. Knowing that my time was limited because of the upcoming light change I knew that if I wanted to say something that now was the time. I looked down from my lofty bus window and said to him very politely, "Sir, I just wanted to let you know that you left your briefcase on your car roof and its open. I thought that you also might want to know that all your papers are blowing all over the place. Have a nice day."

The look on the young man's face went from anger to pure shock and disbelief. I glanced in the buses side mirrors as I drove away and saw the red sports-car parked at the stop and go lights with its emergency flashers on. The angry young man that was driving the red sports car was now frantically running down the street toward the hospital circle picking up his precious papers. I was going to go back and help him pick up all his papers, but; I figured that he didn't want anything to do with me so I didn't. I wondered if that arrogant young man in that red sports car learned anything that day. I know I did.

Chapter 2

Hey look there's a turtle

This medical center circle drive has been a hot spot of memorable events. One Saturday afternoon I pull into the circle drive of the hospital. Saturdays are usually slow and in the late afternoon this medical center is virtually deserted. I had one passenger on the bus and he and I were not talking. I try not to carry on conversations with all my passengers because of safety reasons. I need to concentrate on my driving and pay attention to the road. I was enjoying the quite drive with my only distractions being an occasional interruption of the other driver's communicating with dispatch over the radio. I like an open radio because it keeps me informed of what's going on around the city.

You never know how the passengers are going to react in different situations so the bus driver has to be prepared for anything. As I started to enter the hospital entrance circle my lone passenger starts yelling, "Hey man look at the turtle." I glance in my rear view mirror to see what my passenger is doing. Not knowing what to expect next and being prepared to react and defend myself if needed. I sat there just driving the bus. I glanced into the interior rear view mirror and see my passenger looking out of the side bus window.

My passenger is a younger man perhaps in his mid twenties and appears to be no immediate threat to me. The guy is neatly attired and appears to be normal. He is just staring out of the bus window and is mesmerized by what he is looking at. I can't see what he does because I'm driving the bus. I immediately glance into my side mirrors and see nothing out of the ordinary. I bring the bus to a complete stop because I'm thinking that just maybe he's seeing something that I can't. I was startled at his reactions to whatever he was looking at.

Again he yells, "Look at the turtle." Having to make a comment, I say to him, "you mean the one that's flying out there."

He then gave me a look of disgust and says, "Will you please look at that." I got the sensing that my passenger was serious and was really concerned about whatever he was fixated on. Curiously I watched him as he was pointing out the window toward the outside front door of the bus.

By now my passenger has moved to the front of the bus and is looking out of first window by the first set of seats on my right. He even tried to open the window to get a better look at whatever was out there; but, they were the windows that don't open. I can't see what he is pointing and looking at so, since the bus is stopped anyway, I put my four way flashers on and open the front door of the bus.

Lo and behold, there is a painted turtle just out side the bus door on the circle drive. The turtle is approximately six inches in diameter and maybe 3 inches in height and is just laying there. I look at my passenger and he is just relieved. He was smiling and laughing as he watched the turtle. My opinion of his reaction was that he had proven to me that he wasn't imagining things.

I look at my passenger and say, "go pick the turtle up and put it in the grass before it gets hit by a car or something. He's harmless, he won't bit Yaw." My passenger immediately jumps up from the seat, walks down the front exit stairwell and exits off the bus. He walks up to the turtle and bends over and picks it up. He picked the turtle up as if it were a rock lying on the ground. The only motion that the turtle made was putting its head and legs back into its shell. After picking the turtle up, my bus passenger, with a big grin on his face and turtle in hand, turns toward me to show the turtle to me. The way that my passenger was acting was as if he was a fisherman and had just caught a world record fish. I started to laugh to myself at the way he was acting and his facial expression when he picked the turtle up were hilarious.

My passenger was standing outside of the bus examining his catch, the turtle, as if he never saw a turtle before up close. He was holding the turtle with both of his hands. As he stood there, he was looking around at the surrounding as if he were trying to figure out where he could put the turtle safely out of harms way.

I notice a lady, perhaps in her twenties, who was sitting on a bench up near the front entrance of the hospital. She obviously had a front row seat and was watching the entire turtle ordeal. I watched as the lady threw her book down on the bench, jumped up from her seat on the bench and ran up to the bus passenger holding the turtle. At first I thought that she was going to scold him for picking up the turtle. As she came running up to him she emotionally said, "Thank goodness you caught it, I've been chasing that turtle all day."

My bus passenger looks at me as if asking me what to do. He seems as puzzled as I was by her comment. I told him, "what the heck, give it to her after all she's been chasing it all day."

He gave the turtle to the lady and she graciously thanked him. She seemed very please and started to walk back toward the bench that she had been sitting on. My passenger shook his head in disbelief as he got back on the bus. I'm sure that he was as confused as I was by the young lady's comment about trying to catch it all day. My passenger got on the bus and sat down. I closed the bus door and turned to look at my passenger. We both watched as the lady returned to the bench and sat down. While she was sitting on the bench, she held the turtle out in front of her and was talking to it. My passenger and I were to far away to hear what she was saying to the turtle, but; overall she seemed satisfied and content that someone had finally caught that pesky turtle.

My passenger and I were both seated on the bus now trying to figure out what just had happened. I was getting ready to resume my route. For what ever reason, I looked over at my passenger and we both started laughing uncontrollable. The bus was still parked. It was a couple of minutes before I could compose myself to drive the bus. That male passenger still rides the bus occasionally and he and I get along really well. When ever he gets on the bus, the topic that always comes up is "The lady and the turtle."

I've made my share of little comments to him about that episode that we shared together. I ask him if he thinks that maybe she was Dr. Doolittle and that she was scolding the turtle for playing in the street. He always says to me, "I hope that she doesn't get run over by a heard of stampeding snails." Heaven forbid the comments that come up when he is on the bus and we pass a road kill. It's kind of funny how a little thing like a turtle can get two grown men to act like school yard kids again.

Chapter 3

THE DOLPHIN TRAINER

A lady gets on my bus one afternoon and the first words out of her mouth were, "It stinks like fish on here!" Being the gentleman that I am; there were a dozen comments that I could have made, but I chose a clean one. I knew that there was a young adult, a teenager, seated at the rear of the bus. I immediately made my mind up that if I was going to make a comeback to her comment that my comment had to be clean in nature. I would have to choose my words very carefully not to offend her or the student.

This woman rides the bus a lot and can be a handful at times. She is very opinionated and is not bashful to speak her mind. Many times she'll get on the bus and recite quotes from the bible or just talk about the day's current events. You never know what this lady is going to talk about. The topic is never the same and changes daily. I've convinced myself that she gets her topic of the day from whatever book is available at her doctor's office or where ever she is coming from. This lady has all this information, mostly useless, and she feels that it's her responsibility to report all her findings and beliefs to whomever is driving the bus that day. The woman is usually well dressed and acts very proper. But I really think that it's all a front for the people that she encounters; especially the bus drivers. I sense that she is trying to be someone other than her normal self, but I really don't know that. I would emphatically say that her elevator doesn't actually touch all her floors; if you know what I mean.

I'm a pretty quick thinker and more than often I can come up with a good comeback. One of my mottos is "Don't mess with somebody smarter than you are."

Anyway I'm thinking that I still owe her a comment in response to her fish comment. I look at her, the bus is still stopped with the front door open, and I say spontaneously, "I hope that guy took that bucket of fish with him." I then close the bus door, wait for her to be seated and then start to drive the bus away without saying another word. I knew that the lady was sitting there contemplating about what I had just said. The kid sitting on the back seat of the bus couldn't have cared less what was going on up front because he was listening to his portable CD player.

My inquisitive female passenger sat there for a good two minutes before she responded with a serious, "Why in the world would anybody have a bucket of smelly fish on the bus?" She took the bait, no pun intended, and I jumped on it. I immediately responded with, "You know, that dolphin trainer guy with the beard and little red hat that usually rides the bus. He also wears that wetsuit. Well anyways, I think that he over slept this morning and was running a little late. I'm assuming that he was in a hurry because he had a bucket of stinky fish with him and he never does that."

My female passenger just shook her head up and down in agreement as if she new exactly whom I was talking about. By the way, I don't know of nor do I have any passengers who ride the bus like I just described. Most important, I would never allow someone to bring a bucket of something smelly on my bus.

We live in southeastern Wisconsin and the closest Aquarium to us with dolphins, would probably be Shedds's Aquarium in Chicago which is sixty some miles away. I think that it would be a safe thing to say that any dolphin trainers that they do have working there, most likely would live a little bit closer to the aquarium than in our town.

For the remainder of the bus ride the lady, whom I made those comments to, just sat there contemplating my words. She didn't ask any more questions nor did she strike up any conversation which was fine with me. She seemed content with the explanation that I had given her. That was easier then I thought. She pulled the chime to get off at her normal bus stop. Just before she got off the bus she turned to me and said," when you see that dolphin trainer, you tell him to be more careful with that bucket of fish. Some people don't like that smell." I told her a white lie and said that I would relay her message. Am I bad or what.

She bid me a nice day as she disembarked the bus. I told her to watch her step as she was walking down the stairs. I didn't have the heart to tell her that I was just kidding about the dolphin trainer. Now and then she periodically rides my bus, but she seems a little more subdued with her comments then how she used to be. Every once in a while when she gets on the bus; she'll make a comment about the bus stinking like whatever. But she has never said anything again about the bus stinking like fish. To this day, I have no idea what that lady smelled. Perhaps it was that tuna-fish sandwich that I had for lunch that day. Go figure.

Chapter 4

THE BARF-A-RAMA

What started out as a normal bus ride turned into a memorable experience for at a number of students and me on a beautiful September afternoon a few years ago. I was driving a route which picked up students, or should I say lots of students. The bus that I was driving was forty-four feet long and can carry sixty students safely. I had at least that many middle grade students, teenagers twelve to sixteen, on the bus at the time.

We pick up the students at the local schools with shuttle buses and then bring the students to a central rally point. The central point is usually downtown, where the students then transfer to transit buses whose routes cobweb the city. The kids get home a lot faster that way and it's less of an inconvenience and more economically feasible to the transit department.

On all shuttle or transit buses there is a yellow or white line on the floor extending the width of the aisle just behind the bus driver's area. This line is called the Standee Line. This line is federally mandated and when the bus is in motion no passengers are to be forward of the line. All the passengers that ride the buses that I drive know that I take this safety rule seriously and I will not tolerate anybody breaking it. It is imperative that the bus driver has an unobstructed view and can look out at the road and traffic freely.

I had just left the school and the bus was filled with rowdy, teenaged students. All the seats were filled and the students that were standing, held on to the medal hand-poles; just incase I need to stop suddenly. All the students know to do this from past experiences on the buses. All it takes is for the driver to have to stop suddenly and they all know that someone could get injured if their not hanging on.

As I was driving the crowded bus toward the downtown area, one student came forward of the standee line and stood next to me. I looked at him and was in the process of asking him why he was standing where he was when he interrupted me and said, "I know that I'm not supposed to be standing here; but, I feel sick to my stomach and I feel like I'm going to throw-up." Without hesitation I reached over and handed him my garbage-can. We use the cylindrical plastic containers that coffee comes in as garbage cans because their easy to come by, can be used in numerous situations and are easy to disposed of.

The kid took the plastic coffee container and turned around with the now future up-chuck can in his hands and started to walk toward the rear of the bus. Then it happened. Even though he had the plastic container in his hands, he forgot to use it. Remember now; the bus is crowded with teenagers. The kid, whom had told me that he was going to be sick, was now throwing up on the bus in the crowded aisle amongst his peers. I watched as he did something that I didn't expect him to do, I really figured him to be a lot brighter than what he was going to do next. Instead of him aiming his would be mess toward the empty plastic can that he had in his hands or at least aim at the bus floor; he chose neither. He probably realized after he looked up at the ceiling that that was a rather poor choice for him to make. Actually this was a big mistake on his part. He was a lot shorter than most of the other kids, but; taller than some. He started vomiting on himself more so than on the other students. I know that one of the kids got some on their coat while another got some of it on their pants. Another student, one that I consider lucky, was yelling that they had only gotten on their shoes.

What happened next is what I refer to as a "The puke-a-thon or barf-a rama." At least one other student who I figured couldn't stand the sight of or the smell of his putrid mess; started to vomit on themselves. It looked to me as if vomit was flying everywhere. Now I might be exaggerating a little but I was there and I'm pretty sure what I saw. I got scared. I can tell you that it wasn't a pretty sight.

I glanced in my interior coach mirror and saw what was happening. I use this mirror to keep track of my passengers and what they are doing on the bus, but; never before in my life have I ever saw two kids vomiting so much in such a confined space. I've had kids vomit on the bus before. But never have I had more than one at a time. The odor from the fresh vomit came creeping up on me and the smell was awful. The way the odor approached me was as if it was fog coming onto the shoreline from the ocean depths. I could only imagine that vomit was being spewed everyplace on the bus. My imagination started to go wild. I started to think that vomit was covering the floor, the seats and worst of all, the students. I could only hope that my worst fears weren't coming true. I thought about vomit covered books, folders, coats and knapsacks. I started talking to myself. I know that I said to the kids, "please don't get that stuff on me."

All the students on the bus started yelling and screaming. Some of the kids were yelling at the other kids and some were yelling at me to stop the bus, which I was trying to already do. I pulled into a supermarket parking lot and decide that this was a safe place to stop the bus. I didn't want to make any rash decisions and put anybody getting off the bus in danger, so I again checked out the area that I had stopped at. I put my emergency flashers on, stopped the bus, and set my emergency brake. Only when I knew that it was a safe area did I opened both the front and back doors.

I watched as sixty some students cleared off the bus in what had to be some kind of a record time. Amazingly they did this in an orderly fashion. I was afraid that there was going to be a lot of pushing and shoving when they were exiting the bus; but, there wasn't because nobody wanted to take the chance and get vomit on themselves. Those that had vomit on their person were being careful and considerate and tried not to touch the other passengers. It looked to me as if nobody wanted to touch anyone else. Whatever, it worked for me.

There were books, coats and knapsacks abandoned on the bus as their owners ran for fresh air and freedom. I was the last one, an untouched survivor if I might say, left on the bus. I picked up my radio phone and notified my dispatcher of what had happened. I informed them that I would be running a couple minutes late and that this bus needed a thorough cleaning that night when I returned to the garage. I didn't request another bus because this was my last run of the day.

I had a box of bleach based tidy wipes and a roll of paper towel that I distributed to the kids that had stuck around. The mess wasn't nearly as bad as I thought it was going to be. I told the kids that they didn't need to help me clean the mess up, but they insisted on helping. We all pitched in got the mess cleaned up rather quickly. In reality it wasn't a big mess at all. I notified dispatch and told them that I had just a few kids left on the bus and that they could sit away from the contaminated area. Dispatches response was that if it was OK with kids to ride the bus, that it was OK with them.

There was nothing that we could do to eliminate the stench in the one section of the bus. It seemed to be confined toward the front of the bus. We opened all the bus windows and vents to air the bus out. Most of the sixty or so students chose to walk to the transit center a few blocks away. That left me with just a handful of students on the bus that chose to ride rather than walk to the transfer center.

I used the coffee can that was supposed to be used as the vomit-can to assist in the cleanup. The coffee can was clean and unscathed by any foreign matter; AKA vomit. The students that remained on the bus and myself all had a good laugh and nobody was any worst for the wear. Perhaps, the young man that started it all was a little more embarrassed than the others, but he'll be fine. I do occasionally remind that young man that when he gets on my bus, that under no circumstances is he or any other passengers are allowed to standing in front of the standee line when the bus is in motion.

Chapter 5

CAN YOU TAKE ME TO ALABAMA?

Our transit routes are documented and each driver needs to follow the route and time schedule precisely in order to give our passengers a reliable service. When you are driving a bus, it's OK to be a few minutes late, rather than a few minutes early. Quit a few of the bus rider-ship do not understand the logic behind this. The passengers, who are waiting at the bus stop, become impatient if the bus is running a few minutes behind and they will call the transit dispatcher with their cell phones. Most of the time the passenger and dispatcher are talking on the phone when the bus pulls up to the bus stop. I understand perfectly the passengers concerns. They depend on the local transit system to get them to where ever they need to go. The passengers concerns are valid because many times a bus runs what we drivers call "HOT". In a nutshell all this terminology means is that the bus is not at the same location that is posted on the bus schedule. If we drivers do need to deviate from the prescribed routes or we know that were running "Hot" we need to notify our dispatcher immediately. This is especially important if we are scheduled to meet up with other buses at transfer points. Route deviations occur for different reasons;

accidents, road construction, weather or sometimes customer courtesy stops.

I remember one passenger who got on the bus the day after Thanksgiving Day. This day is the busiest shopping day of the year because of the start of the holiday season. We typically have literally ten times the passenger volume than we normally do on any given day. The shopping centers are packed with people and cars. Shoppers are more concerned about getting into the stores to get a bargain than they are about their personal safety. It's like people walking lose all their common sense. They walk in front of the buses and cars with no fear of getting run over by them. Cars drive through the plaza parking lots looking for parking places and forget that their driving a vehicle. I would say that I've witnessed more minor traffic accidents in the parking lots on this day of year than any other day. I think the next busiest and hectic day for the transit systems would be the day after Christmas. Yea, this is the day when people return those unwanted or broken Christmas presents.

So anyway this man was standing by the bus stop. He appeared to be a middle aged shorter man and was causally dressed. I actually thought that he was under dressed because, aside from the normal pants and shirt, he was just wearing a light sports coat. I don't know why I thought he was under dressed, what the heck, quit a few of the kids are still wearing shorts and cutoffs. In our area at this time of year the weather can change drastically within an hour. The weather could be in the mid sixties in the early afternoon and by supper time it could be snowing.

Hey, I'm Marty. I drive the bus

The man who was about to board my bus, was holding a medium sized multicolored suitcase in one hand and a dollar bill in his other. I pulled the bus up to the bus stop and opened the front door. The man immediately came toward the bus and hastily walked up the two steps toward me. He looked as if he were on a mission and that he needed to get someplace fast. The man was now within a two feet of me and stood by the fare box. I kept my eye on him because I wasn't sure what his intentions were. I watched as he hastily set his suitcase down on the bus floor. In one motion he reached toward me with his hand that had the dollar bill in as if to give the money to me. I then noticed that the bill in his hand that he was trying to give me was not a dollar bill as I originally though it was, but rather; a twenty dollar bill.

I sat there in the bus seat trying to comprehend what this guys intentions were and why was he trying to hand me money. I don't take any money from passengers; that is why there is a fare box on the bus. Secondly, bus drivers don't give change. I was just about to tell the man that and looked up toward his face. He was staring me straight in the eyes and said, "Can you take me to Alabama? I've got a lot more money."

I explained to him that our transit system was local and that we usually don't do stuff like that; but, I'll call my dispatcher and see what they say. I knew that we were going to help this guy out, but I wasn't quite sure how yet. I also knew exactly what the answer was going to be from my dispatcher when I asked them if I could deviate about six hundred miles from my route and go to Alabama. Now remember were located in Wisconsin. What the heck, I'm sure that by me asking a question like that would add a little more spice to the transit system radio waves. The radio was already buzzing because of the hectic shopping day, so me thinking of how I was going to word my radio request was really a none issue. I figured that I'd wing it and called dispatch to have some fun with my passengers request.

I got on the radio called my bus number and waiting for dispatch response. When my response was answered I questioned my dispatcher if it would be OK for me to deviate from my route for a day or two and put an extra thirteen hundred miles on the bus by going round trip to Alabama. Their response was, "What, could you please repeat what you just said." I did and the radio went silent. I had an open radio which means that most of the other drivers could hear my radio transmissions and I could hear theirs. There was nothing but silence. I knew that they were all listening to our conversation.

I continued to drive my route as I waited for dispatched response. Meanwhile the passenger that had inquired about the ride home to Alabama sat patiently in the front seat of the bus, clutching his suitcase, waiting for an answer. In all the confusion I forgot to charge the man for the bus ride. I told him that I had to charge him a dollar and that I would probably be giving him a transfer for another bus. I waited for a minute or so and still no response from dispatch. I figured that I better straighten this out before I get in hot water. I radioed dispatch and he answered sarcastically, "We're working on your last request, please give us time." I said to him, "Maybe what I'll do is transfer this fellow to route four, this route goes to the train station, and he can take the Metro-train to Chicago. He would have a much better chance to find a bus or train there that would take him to Alabama than from here don't you think?" I was speaking to my dispatcher rather quickly because I now really wanted to end these radio transmissions.

My dispatcher said that that was a much better Idea than my first one was. I informed the Alabamian passenger that my dispatcher informed me through telepathic communications that there was no way that my bus or I could not accommodate him by bringing him to Alabama. The passenger gave me a funny look as if he didn't understand what I had just said. Wanting to clear up any miscommunications that I might have caused I informed the passenger that I had an alternate plan for him to get home. This alternate plan would save him some money, get him to Alabama in a timely manner and more importantly help me keep my job. He thought that my alternate plan was a great idea and that he would use it and travel that way. He thanked me for taking the time to help him. I told him that I was just doing my job. In a way I was kind of bummed out because it would have been a nice break for me to help this fellow out and drive to the southern states. I knew that the weather forecast for upcoming days called for snow.

When I got back to the transit garage that evening the other drivers told me that they were hoping for a go ahead from dispatch for me to take that fellow to Alabama. I knew why, because if dispatch would have allowed me go to Alabama; the other drivers could maybe accommodate passengers, who request to go to Florida next winter.

Chapter 6

BREAST FEEDING ON THE BUS

When I'm driving the bus I try to keep tract of everything that is going on around me. This includes inside and outside of the bus. While I'm driving on a route I scan the road in front of me to help me keep tract of traffic and obstacles that I may encounter. One of the greatest benefits of doing this is that I can see if I have passengers waiting up ahead to get on the bus. One day while I was driving and doing my normal scan, I saw people standing at the next bus stop. As I pulled the bus over to the curb near the bus stop, standing there waiting to catch the bus was what appeared to be a family of four. There was a man; a woman; a young child about three years old; and an infant baby that lady was carrying.

I opened the front doors of the bus and the man got on the bus first. As he was walking up the steps he asked me if the young child had to pay. I told him if the child was under age five year that there was not a charge for him. The then put two adult fares into the fare box. As he turned and started to walk toward the rear of the bus he said to me, "That's for me and my wife. The kids are free."

I said to him,"OK, that's fine." By now the young boy had gotten on the bus and was standing next to him by the standee line. The man took the child by the hand and led him toward the rear of the bus. I glance up into the interior mirror just to see where they were going to sit. Not that it really mattered, I just like to keep tract of where I have passengers seated.

I turned my head toward the open front doors and watched as the man's wife started up the bus steps. Knowing that she had an infant in her arms, I wanted to tell her to watch her step. I never got the words out of my mouth. As she walked up the last of three steps up into the bus and was standing near me; I just sat there gawking at her. When you're a bus driver nothing that your passengers do really surprises you, but; I was surprised.

That was the first time that I noticed that she was breastfeeding the infant. It caught me off guard as I watched the infant suckling on his mother's, might I add, very exposed breast. She asked me something about the baby paying or something, but; I was mesmerized and just sat there watching the infant enjoying his meal. I said, "OK whatever. Uh, your husband took care of it." I don't usually get lost for words, but needless to say, I was. I was a little setback, and I didn't want to make myself appear like a fool or pervert. Even though I was thinking that, I was positive that she saw that I was gawking at her. The lady turned toward the rear of the bus and went to sit down.

I tried to remember what the transit policy was on breast feeding, but; no matter how hard I thought about that, I couldn't get that image of that infant sucking on his mother's breast out of my mind. The bus was still parked by the bus stop. I turned in my seat and curiously watched as she walked causally in the coach of the bus. I watched in the mirror as the lady sat down in a seat near her husband and other child. Of course the seat that she chose was in front of her husband and perfectly lined up with my interior mirror. Like I need that kind of distraction; you know what I mean. I composed myself and pulled the bus away from the curb and into the traffic flow. Mom and dad and the kids were the only passengers on the bus. Man was I grateful for that.

As I drove the bus, I noticed the mother fumbling through a baby bag that she had with her. She was still exposed as she took a small blanket out the bag. I never notice that she had a bag with her when she boarded the bus. She then placed the blanket over the baby head, covering what was going on. I was ecstatic when she did that. I thought that the worst was over now and I could continue driving without any interruptions. I was wrong. The baby, maybe out of exuberance of the nutritional value of the meal or instinctive self indulgence, started making very loud sucking and slobbering sounds. I tried not to look in the mirror, but; couldn't help myself. The sounds that the infant was making annoyed me. It annoyed me in way that I thought of it as rather funny. The noises reminded of a fish feeding frenzy that I watched on the discovery channel the night before.

Mom was enjoying the scenery of the bus ride with an occasional winching of her body and a grimacing look on her face. I wouldn't say that she was in pain, but; rather enduring what she had to do. Dad and the little boy paid no attention to what was happening a few feet away. Just part of life I guess.

I said to myself, "Just drive the bus and keep looking forward and forget about it." I did so even though I could still hear the infant's slobbering sucks.

I thought to myself, "What am I going to do if someone else gets on the bus and they have objections with the lady breastfeeding?" I figured that I had enough to deal with now and would deal with that predicament if it should come up. Until that happens, I wasn't going to worry about it.

About twelve blocks away the long awaited chime rang signaling a request to stop the bus. My only passengers were the aforementioned family and I was ecstatic. I pulled the bus out of traffic and stopped the bus at the curb near the bus stop. I put my flashers on and opened the front doors, than I waited for the family to disembark. As the family was getting off the bus, the dad and little boy walked past me first. The dad thanked me for the safe bus ride and commented about my punctuality as he was getting off the bus. I graciously acknowledged his comments and told him to have a nice day.

The little boy was holding his dad hand and looking at me. He was waiting for me to say something to him. So, not wanting to disappoint him; I gestured my hand in a waving motion to him said to him, "See ya later pal. You come and ride the bus again, OK." He smiled and wave back to me as he gleefully got off the bus.

The mother, holding the now fed infant in her arms, walked past me and stopped at the top step of the stairwell. She turned toward me and said, "I want to thank you for allowing me to breast feed my baby on the bus. I apologize for any inconvenience that I may have caused you. Thank you for your professionalism. I only wish that I had realized that I had that extra blanket with me sooner."

I thought to my self," Yea, me too lady."

As she turned to walk down the bus steps, I said, "have a nice day and please watch your step." She gestured a wave toward me as she got off the bus and walked toward her waiting husband. The now assembled family stood there watching as I pulled the bus away from the curb. The delighted little boy was waving his upraised arm telling me bye. I waved back as I drove away.

After they were gone and I had resumed my route, I immediately called my route supervisor and asked what transit policy was on breast feeding. He said that he really didn't know offhand and that he would get back to me shortly. I told him no big rush now. He got back to me in a timely manner, within minutes, with an answer. It seems that I handled the situation properly. I guess keeping quiet can be a good thing at times.

The only thing that I wish is that the next time a mom has to breast feed her infant on my bus is that the mom remembers that she has an extra blanket in the bag before she gets on the bus.

Chapter 7

Lady please keep your clothes on!!

Along the same line of thought, I'm reminded of an incident that happened on a hot, steamy, humid August evening. It was the last run of the day for me and I was looking forward to parking the bus and going home. Although the bus is air conditioned, the opening and closing of the front door from letting passengers on and off the bus all day exposed me to the fluctuating temperatures around me. The temperature and humidity outside of the bus was very hot and humid, while the temperature inside of the bus was very cool. I think that combination was the catalyst of an extremely bad headache that I was experiencing most of the day.

I picked up a lone passenger about two minutes into my route. As she entered the bus and flashed her bus pass toward me; she was complaining about the weather. My head was pounding and I said to myself as she was talking to me, "Yea lady. Like you're the first one today to tell me how hot it is outside." Not wanting to appear unfriendly toward her; I nodded my head in agreement with her as she passed by me. I also said to her, "you ain't kidding it's a warm one."

She was one of the local hotel workers. Not to long ago when she was riding on my bus she told me that she was a cleaning woman. I know that this woman works quit a few hours a day and always goes to work. I've never had any kind of problem with her when she's on the bus and she is always friendly. She has a pleasant personality. I figure her age to be in the mid-thirties. She doesn't usually ride my bus, but; she has a bus pass and is more than welcome to ride. I always wait until my passengers get to their chosen seats before I move the bus. You know; safety reasons. I waited as she headed toward the rear seat of the bus. As she walked toward the rear seat she was saying something to me about her back hurting and that she needed to get home.

I told her to grab a seat. I also told to her that I was more than happy to accommodate her request because I wanted to go home too. She nodded in agreement and sat down on the rear seat of the bus.

I resumed with my route knowing that I would be off duty in a little while and going home. It was some consolation to look forward to anyhow. My head was pounding and I just wanted this day to be over. When I drive the bus, I continuously use both my interior mirrors and exterior mirrors for obvious safety reasons. As I casually glanced into my interior rear view mirror scanning the coach of the bus; I saw something that startled me and caught me completely off guard. I saw the image of a naked woman in the mirror. As I looked in bewilderment at the reflection in the mirror, I'm not really believing what I seeing, Still driving the bus, I glance back toward the mirror and realize that the woman was not completely naked, just naked from the waist up. I very loudly exclaimed, "What the heck is going on back there!"

The cleaning woman, my lone passenger, immediately looked toward the front of the bus. As her eyes met my eyes in the mirror and she hysterically exclaimed, "Oh my God, I so sorry."

I said, "Lady, would please refrain from taking your clothes off while you're on the bus." She emphatically insisted, "That her bra was killing her and that she needed to get it off." I interrupted her and said, "I don't care! Please, next time take it off at home." I was starting to get angry at her. I regained my senses and decided that the best thing that I could do was to keep my mouth shut and just drive the bus.

Frustrated with her actions, I continued to drive the bus. I tried to make sense of what she was doing and why she was doing it on my bus. I again glanced toward the mirror and noticed that the lady now was dressed and had her blouse back on. One feature that we have on the buses is interior cameras. There are four cameras strategically placed to view potential problematic areas on the buses. And this situation was defiantly one of them. I'm thinking to myself that I hope the cameras are picking this up just incase this lady didn't like how I handled the situation.

As we drove on she came up to the front of the bus and sat down in a seat just to my right and said, "I'm really sorry, I didn't think that you would see me." That's when I calmly told her, "Lady, we have cameras on the buses that record everything that is said and done." I then pointed them out to her. She looked at the cameras and said, "Oh well."

I continued with my route and she sat there looking at me wanting to say something. I think that she was about to cry. I know that women always cry when they think something bad is going to happen. I needed to say something, I said, "Please don't do that again."

She very sheepishly said, "You're not going to call the cops are you?" I said, "No, but I'm going to have to write an incident report and talk to my supervisor about what happened."

We drove on and continued the route. I had just driven a few blocks when she pulled the chime line indicating that she wanted me to stop at the next stop. I pulled up to the curb near the bus stop to drop her off. As she disembarked she turned to me and said, "Do what you have to do I understand, but, I really am sorry and I promise that I won't ever do anything like that on the bus again." After she said that she started to cry and got off the bus. I felt sorry for what had happened. I pulled the bus away from the curb and finished my route.

When got back to the transit garage, I spoke to my supervisor about the incident and how I thought that the lady was truly sorry. I reminded him that it was one of those days that the heat could drive a person to do irrational things. He agreed, but; he claimed that in the public interest he would reserved his final answer until he reviewed the tape of the incident. I also suggested to him that we act very discrete and show some compassion. I really believe that the heat made her act the way she did.

He told me that he would have the tape pulled from the buses camera and recorder just in case something does arise from the incident. He stated that he would view the tape and the recordings to insure that I handled myself professionally. He also recommended that I write an incident report to get my accounts of the incident if needed in the future. I wrote the report.

It was several weeks before I saw the lady again. As she boarded the bus; I could tell by her kinesics that she recognized me as the driver of the bus from our last encounter on that hot, humid, sultry August evening. I bid her good morning as she showed me her current monthly bus pass. She nodded her head in acknowledgement of my comment. Not making eye contact with me she turned toward the rear of the bus and started to walk toward the unoccupied seats. I had other passengers on the bus and didn't want to embarrass anyone, especially myself, with an inappropriate unprofessional comment. The lady stopped walking and turned toward me. She made eye contact with me and very seriously said, "Thank you."

I'm not a mind reader, but; I knew exactly what she meant when she said that. It was her way of saying that she would keep her blouse on and not take her bra off while riding on my bus.

I respectfully replied with a gracious, "You're welcome." I guess that's my way of saying to her, I would appreciate that very much.

Chapter 8

LARGE SCARY GUY AND THE DOLLAR BILL

Driving the bus is a people watching experience. There is this one fellow, who will remain nameless, that is perhaps one of the scariest individuals whom I've ever encountered. I'm not stereo-typing this fellow, but; I'm sure I saw him on some late night scary movie wielding an ax and chasing people around. This guy is almost seven feet tall and weighs approximately three hundred pounds or so. Although he has an athletic appearance and is muscle bound; this individual is extremely uncoordinated. He dresses very conservatively and is penny-wise.

The personality traits and mannerisms of this individual dramatically change day to day. I know that these traits are normal of everyone, but not to the extremes that this fellows' are. One day he is friendly as can be; while, the next day he gives you a scary piercing stare and won't say a word to you.

Again I need to come back to reality and to remind myself that there are reasons why people ride the bus. I need to keep reality in perspective by reinforcing myself and my values by insisting that this is a job and I'm not here to judge my rider-ship, but rather; to drive the bus.

Hey, I'm Marty. I drive the bus

On a rather windy, rainy autumn day this huge fellow was waiting at his usual bus stop. As I pulled up I noticed that he was intensely looking at what appeared to be a dollar bill. He was holding the dollar bill with his thumb and index finger of each hand cinched tightly in its corners. The dollar actually appeared small compared to the size of his baseball mitt sized hands. He stood there holding the dollar bill approximately twelve to fifteen inches in front of his face and was staring at it as if he were trying to decipher it or something on it. It didn't appear that he saw the bus pulling up and I was not going to take a chance of him stepping out and getting hurt, so I slowed the bus down.

As I pulled up in front of him I was feathering my brakes to stop the bus. I was about five yards away from him when the dollar bill that he was holding, somehow flew out of his hands. I'm sure that it wasn't the air brakes on my bus that caused the rush of air, but; rather just a sudden gust of wind. All that I really remember is that he gave me a piercing look as if I had done something wrong. I looked at him and shrugged my shoulders and gestured with my hands that I didn't do anything. You know what I mean like when you put your arms in front of you and show your palms up like you're surrendering to somebody.

By now the dollar bill was being blown down the street and this rather large fellow was now in hot pursuit after it. As he was running down the street after his wind blown dollar, he kept glancing back at the bus toward me. It was as if he was trying to communicate telepathically with me. I understood his message perfectly. He wanted to ride the bus, but; he had to catch that elusive dollar bill first. I knew that, remember I'm the one who pulled the bus over to the curb to pick him up.

I watched at his fruitless labors. Every time he bent over to pick up his dollar, the wind would catch it and make it float just out of his grasp. He tried numerous times to stepping on the dollar. That was a sight to see, but; it didn't work either. The dollar, no matter how hard this huge fellow tried, kept moving away from his efforts to grab it or step on it. Every time he was unsuccessful in grabbing the dollar, he would glance back at the bus. I could tell that he was becoming more and more agitated. I was thinking to myself that maybe he is blaming me and my big stupid bus for him having to run after his precious dollar bill. This changed everything. The issue at hand was now becoming serious.

I could see that he was really getting frustrated and I was in actuality starting to worry about the situation. I was worried that he was thinking that I did something to cause his torment. Not only that, I was thinking also that he might decide to let the wind have the dollar as long as he could catch me. You need to remember the fact that this guy is huge. I didn't want him to take his frustrations out on me or my bus. Heck if worst came to worst, he could have the bus. I started thing irrational about what could happen. It seemed that my greatest concern on hand now was that my bus was going to stall as I'm trying to drive away, trying to save my precious insignificant life.

Some psychological experts believe that when you have a near death experience; that your life flashes before you. I would agree with them. That was the only time in my life when my present life and my past reincarnated stages of life's past before my eyes. This was the time when I found out that I was actually reincarnated as an Egyptian boat rower. Even though I thought the situation was serious and I was hallucinating, it was hilarious watching this guy trying up to catch that dollar. It's funny how things happen right in front of you when you don't have a camrecorder available. I'm sure that this would have won me some money on America's funniest home videos show. Oh well.

Finally the pursued dollar bill landed in a rather large, muddy puddle of water. The dollar's brief freedom flight had finally come to an end. The big fellow was so intent on getting that dollar; I really think he was possessed by it, that getting wet didn't matter to him. He took his size twelve or so shoe and stomped on the dollar bill. When he did that the dollar went under the water and out of sight. He had finally corralled the elusive dollar, but; he also got something that he didn't count on. That was getting soaked from the waist down from the water splashing up from his foot stomping down.

He reached down in the water with his rather large hand and came up with his wind blown fortune. He glared at the dollar, now in his custody, and was muttered something to it. As he put the now drenched dollar bill into his pocket he seemed to be talking to it. I was about twenty yards away from him and seated in the bus so I couldn't hear a word that he was saying. I could just see his lips moving. I was petrified.

He was wearing a light colored jacket and I could see that the sleeve of that jacket was now soaked to the mid forearm. Standing in the puddle, the man glanced down at his drenched pants and wet coat sleeve. He paused for a moment or so as if he were thinking of what to do next. His mixed thoughts must have turned toward the bus because he quickly turned his head as if to check and see if the bus was still waiting for him. It was.

I thought that this was it for me. I hope he didn't see me chuckling when he was having the footrace, but; with my luck he did and now I'm going to get an earful or worse.

As the huge wet fellow lumbered up to the bus, I sat there thinking to myself, "well I've led a good life, things could have been worst." You know the stuff you say just before you meet your maker.

The man now stood outside the closed front door of the bus looking at me with that piercing stare. I felt a little safe and secure with the buffer of the closed bus doors between the two of us. The sound of the bus engine running was also gave me a false sense of courage, but: not that much. I had the front doors of the bus closed because technically there was nobody at the bus stop when I had stopped. Remember, he left and was running down the road away from the bus chasing the dollar. So, I really didn't have any good reason to have the bus doors open. After all it was raining outside. To be quite frank with you, I was really scared and not thinking rationally.

Knowing that sooner or later that I had to open the doors; I figured that now was as good as time as any. I opened the bus doors, against my better judgment, and prepared for the worst. The large, wet, scary man stood not more four feet away staring directly at me. I just sat there in the bus seat, cowering not saying a word, just waiting anticipating the end.

I was pleasantly surprised and relieved when the large man calmly and rationally said to me, "Thank you for waiting, sir. I need to go home and change my clothes because I got wet. I'll catch the next bus. See yaw later buddy."

I was a very disappointed about the entire situation. I was disappointed with myself that I blew that situation out of proportion with my idle ramblings; I was disappointed that I stereotyped and prejudged this fellow because of his unusual appearance; but more so, I was disappointed because I didn't have a working cam recorder with me. Maybe next time.

I responded to his comment with a pleasant and grateful, "have a nice day." Talk about being relieved. It's funny how your mind can play tricks on you isn't it.

I see that rather large fellow occasionally and I try not to think about the ordeal that he went through, but: every time I do see him, I think about that memorable day. I recall him running; the dollar bill floating and that big mud puddle splashing. I get a smile on my face and have a good laugh to myself. After all he did call me his buddy.

Every once in a while when I'm sitting on the bus at the end of the line daydreaming, thinking about whatever, that ordeal comes to mind. My bus passengers give me peculiar looks and ask me; what's so funny? My response to them is, "Did you ever have an out of body life and death experience."

Marty Molinaro

Most of my passengers know my sense of humor and just ignore me. Those passengers that don't know me; well, they look at me like I've lost it and just go on with their busy lives. One way or another I don't care, after all; what do I know, I just drive the bus.

Chapter 9

Twenty dollar bill in Traffic

Talking about money; one day I'm stuck in afternoon traffic waiting for the light to turn green. I have a bus full of passengers and I am running a few minutes behind schedule. I need to arrive downtown at the transfer center within a certain time-frame so that my passengers can make the connecting transfers to other buses that are gathering there. Once my passengers get at the transfer center, they will link up with other transit buses that will take them to various sections of the city. Likewise, I will have transfers from those other buses with passengers wanting to go to where my route travels.

Weekday afternoons around here from three thirty to about five thirty are usually very hectic. Just like anyplace else; commuters are making there journey home. Rather than say hectic, I probably should say busier than normal. Around here we don't have what you would call traffic jams, compared to what I've experienced in say Chicago or Milwaukee. There are times when construction or traffic accidents do delay traffic temporarily.

As I'm sitting in the bus, watching the traffic not move and the traffic light not change, something catches my eye. On the ground, in front of the bus and in the street was a twenty dollar bill. I watch as the wind gathers the twenty and puts it in flight. As it goes blowing by the front of the bus; I'm thinking, hey free money! I'm not positive, but; I think that the portrait of Andrew Jackson winked at me as he was passing by. I watch as the twenties flight takes it under the car parked next to me in traffic. I want to make that twenty dollar bill mine, but; my problem is, how do I drive the bus and at the same time chase the twenty though standing traffic.

The wind was blowing and the twenty came out of the other side of the parked car. I know that because the twenty was floating in the air as I sat there watching helplessly. I'm sure other drivers waiting in traffic have seen it by now. Nobody in there right mind is going to step into traffic for a twenty dollars right? Wrong!

It appeared to me that the twenty had come from the service s station located immediately to my right. That's when I become aware of, or thought that I established, the twenty dollar bills rightful owner. I assume that because of the way that this guy was acting in the parking lot of the service station. He was frantically looking around as if he had lost something. I was sure that I knew exactly what he was looking for.

It's amazing what chances people will take for money. Heck if only my bus door had been open when the twenty came blowing by, maybe it would have blown into my bus, on my lap and the story would have been over. Nope, that didn't happen. One thing was for sure, that guy in the service station parking lot wanted his money back.

Let me tell you about this guy. He was in his mid thirties and well dressed. He appeared to be quite agile and athletic as he ran from the safety of the service station drive and into standing traffic. He was talking to himself and appeared to be cussing. I've seen individuals throwing little hissy fits and he was definitely having one. At the same time that he was having this emotional setback; he was keeping track of which way the wind was blowing.

He looked to me like he might have been a lawyer or in some other professional position. I don't know how much education he had because he sure lacked common sense. I was quit obvious to me that his mama never taught him not to play in the street amongst the traffic.

I glanced over at the service station and the only car that was there was a little red sports car. I think that it was a beamer (BMW). I started to recall some of the experiences that I've had in the past with a little red sports car and its belligerent driver. I was absolutely positive that this was the same individual and the same red sports car that had crossed paths with me before in a driveway at a medical complex. The car was parked at the gas pump and the driver's door was wide open. I instinctively looked to see if there was an open briefcase on the roof of the red sports car for reasons that I really don't know. I was positive that this was where this twenty dollar bill caper had originated.

About now my bus passengers were talking about, quote: "the idiot running around the cars in the street." I have a front row seat and can see everything. The traffic light was still red and this guy was bending over looking under the parked cars, in the middle of the street, looking for the twenty dollar bill. Other vehicle drivers who saw the guy in the street started honking their horns at him. I don't know if they were honking at him to get his attention to tell him where the twenty was or were honking at him to tell him to get out of the street. He didn't care about them; he was on a mission. He wanted that money. As he continued looking for the money, and the cars would honk at him, he would raise his hand and give the middle finger to whoever had honked their car horns. I know for sure now that this was the same guy I encountered not to long ago. There seems to be a correlation between him giving the finger to drivers and driver's honking their vehicles horns at him. I really don't think that this guy enjoyed the sounds of car, truck or especially bus horns by his predictable reaction.

The guy was frantically bending over looking under all the cars. As I watched him, I could see the twenty dollar bill floating in the air a good thirty feet from where he was looking. So being the concerned guy I am, I honked the bus horn. I than yelled to him out of my driver's window and said, "Hey man, your twenty just got blown in the east bound lanes. Get out of the street before you get killed."

He stopped and stared at me and gave me a look as if he knew me. I guess you could say that we knew each other. He than raised his arm and gave me the middle finger. I'm sure that this guy now recognized me as the bus driver who tried to tell him about his briefcase not to long ago. Obviously he's didn't learn anything from that experience either. Being the professional that I am, I just sat there and watched.

Other drivers and myself watched as the guy, who was chasing the money, headed toward the east bound traffic lanes. About that time, a semi truck pulling a fifty three foot trailer came thundering by. As the truck and trailer passed by the twenty dollar bill went with the truck. I literally mean went with the truck. An air flow was created as the truck and trailer passed causing paper and other debris to follow the rig as if it were a vortex. The twenty dollar bill was sucked up under the big rig and disappeared. Where it went I had no idea.

By now the traffic light had changed green and traffic was starting to flow. The motorist's, that were waiting for the light to change; were now keeping an eye on this guy standing in the street because nobody knew he was doing or going to do next. The oncoming traffic from the east was slowing down because this guy was now in their lanes of traffic. I myself was figuring that he was going to start running after the big rig and trailer to retrieve the twenty.

One elderly female motorist must have thought that this guy was a thief or car-jacker. I watched as she was reached over and locked her passenger side door. The lady was screaming at the man as the he stood there watching her. He just shook his head and looked at her. As she drove off she gave him the middle finger and cursed him out. I guess what goes around comes around. I watched the guy as he helplessly stood there watching as the elderly woman, the big truck and his twenty drove away. He also was acting a little sheepish and reserved from I would guess being scolded by the elderly woman. I think that she hurt his ego. Good for her, she did something that I was trying to do.

The bus was still parked as traffic was starting to move around the bus. While this was going on, my first thought was, "I hope this guy gets out of the road before somebody hits him."

It must have dawned on him where he was and how idiotic he was acting over a twenty dollar bill. I still had my emergency flashers on and had the bus stopped. I was stopped because I didn't know where or what this guy was going to do next. My opinion was that he was acting like a fool and now its time for him to go home. During the incident, he was acting very irrational and was very inconsiderate to all of those around him. That seemed to be normal for this guy. All I knew for sure was that I wasn't going to be the one that was going to run him over with the bus and lose my job over his stupidity.

Traffic started to move a little faster and he headed back from where he had come from, the service station. Obviously he was giving up his chase for the twenty dollar bill. Cars were still honking at him, but; he was ignoring them. I'm sure all he wanted to do now was to get back to his car. After a few close calls, he made it back safely to his parked car.

I watched as he got in his red sports car and started to drive away. As he exited the driveway of the service station, he pulled out in front of the bus and cut me off. I just shook my head and watched. I guess that he did this as if to show me that he could do what he wanted to do. His actions didn't faze me a bit. I continued with my route and made it downtown on schedule.

I often wondered if that guy who was chasing that twenty had lost it or if he saw it blowing by and wanted to make it his. Any way you look at it; him running after it into traffic, was an unintelligent thing for him to do.

I drive that route occasionally and when I do; I think about that twenty dollar bill. Since I witnessed that ordeal that day, I find that when I'm in that area and driving the bus or my private vehicle that, I drive just a little bit slower. Also when I am driving east on that street, I find that I automatically pull to the far right lane and slow down drastically looking for anything that might resemble that twenty dollar bill. As far as I know that twenty is still hooked up with that big rig and going down the road to who knows where.

Chapter 10

MY HOME IS IN HEAVEN

Like I say there are many reasons that people ride the bus and I try not to really get involved. My mom taught me to treat people like you want them to treat you and this often is a stumbling block for me. I try to use common sense and do the right thing when I'm dealing with my passengers. One day I pulled into the shopping plaza at the south end of my route. As I pulled up to the bus stop there was a young man, perhaps in his mid twenties, standing and waiting for the bus.

I pulled the bus up to the bus-stop and I noticed that the young man was looking at me and crying. I opened the front doors of the bus and waited for him to board the bus. He just stood there in front of the open doors looking at me and crying.

I said to the guy, "you getting on the bus?" He didn't move and just stood there looking at me.

I waited a few seconds and asked him again, "Are you getting on the bus or what?"

He replied, "I have an injury to my leg and I don't have any money. I need to get to near down town and I can't walk that far." He just stood there looking at me waiting to see what my reply would be. A few seconds passed and I felt sorry for the guy. Not knowing or asking where near downtown he was going; I told him to get on the bus and I'll cover his fare this time, but; only this time. I usually carry extra change just incase situation like this come up. You would be surprised, the number of people that want to ride the bus and don't have any money. I don't mind helping people out, but; I will not be taken advantage of.

I put the money in the fare-box and he thanked me. He really seemed as if he appreciated what I was doing for him. I never saw this guy before and I don't believe that he ever rode on any buses that I had driven, but: I could be wrong. He seemed like a rather pleasant guy, but; there was something about him that I didn't like. I'm not sure what that was. As he got on the bus I noticed that he walked with a pronounced hobble. After boarding, he proceeded toward the rear of the bus and sat down on the rear seats. I closed the bus doors and continued with my route.

I was feeling pretty good about helping this guy out, but; I also had a little guilty feeling. Why, I don't know. Not knowing the whole story, I was wondering to myself, "What on earth was going though this guy's mind that would make him cry? Maybe something to do with his leg, I don't know."

Coming back to reality, I said to myself, "Mind your own business and drive the bus. Yaw did a good thing now forget about it"

As I continued with my route I kept a watchful eye on my lone passenger. He seemed to be enjoying the bus ride and was contently watching the scenery passing by. He propped his bad leg up on the seat and was just sitting there. He had stopped crying and had composed himself.

I never really gave him a second thought until we got near downtown.

I arrived at the midpoint of the route, downtown, and announced our location over the loudspeaker. My lone passenger nodded his head to acknowledge that he understood my message. I watched as he looked out of the window and acted as if he was figuring out where we were.

Our city bus routes are setup so each bus route has two ends and a mid point. The midpoint is always the transfer center downtown. This is where all the buses congregate. Each of the transit routes have north and south legs or east and west legs. Routes take twenty five minutes to one half hour to complete a leg. Traffic and the weather usually determine the length of time to complete a route leg. One leg is considered driving from the transfer center, mid-point, to the far end of any designated route.

I need to say that there are a few routes that do go out to numerous industrial parks and outlying shopping centers. These routes vary in time and are the exception to rules. When these routes were created, they were designated to transport workers to and from their jobs.

At the transfer center the drivers can take a little break and use the facilities if necessary. At the end of the route leg there are usually facilities available for the driver to use because the legs more that likely end at shopping malls, Service station plazas, schools or nursing homes.

When I got downtown, I got off the bus to stretch my legs and take a little walk. Every driver does something different while their waiting at transfer points. I enjoy talking with the other drivers. I think that I do that because it gives me a different perspective of my job. I was talking with a few other drivers and mentioned to them about the guy that I picked up who was standing at the bus stop crying. I then added that he had a bum leg too. One of the other drivers immediately said that he vaguely remembered an incident, not to long ago, about a guy from Chicago using a similar ploy to get free rides on our buses.

I told the other driver, "naw, it couldn't be this guy because it seemed as if he was really distressed." As our little gathering broke up, I told my buddies that I would keep an eye on this guy and let them know what happens.

I got back on the bus and started the second leg of my route. I then noticed that the guy, that was crying, was still on my bus. I figured that maybe he was new in town and was using the transfer center to kind of get his bearing. In retrospect, I guess that I was fooling myself and making excuses for him. As I headed to the north side of town, I figured to myself that he would be getting off any time now. As it was, I reached the end of the route leg. I drove the entire leg of the route and the guy who needed to get near downtown obviously had no intention of getting off the bus. Maybe this was the same guy that my fellow driver had warned me about.

I stop the bus at the end of the route and walk to the rear of the bus. I say to the guy, "Hey Pal, I did you a favor giving you a ride. You can't ride the bus all day. Where do you need to get off and where do you live?"

At that he looked me in the face and smiled sarcastically. He then said, "My home is in heaven." When he said that, I knew right then and there that I had been duped. Heck, this bus doesn't go there. I tried to give this guy a break and help him, and he was taking advantage of me and my generosity. Needless to say I was irritated with my new found friend. I do not like to be bamboozled by anyone. I thought to myself,"So, he thinks that he can come here from Chicago and take advantage of our hospitality, huh, we'll see about that."

My response to him was, "This bus doesn't go there, but: I got a special place where I can drop you off." He gave me a kind of puzzled look and said, "OK. Wherever you drop me off will be fine with me just as long as I don't have to walk too far because of my bum leg."

I said to him, "Don't worry about that Pal, I got just the place for ya." I live on the north side of town near the end of the bus route leg where we were and I sure didn't want to drop this guy off near my house and perhaps have to maybe put up with him later. I sat there thinking to myself as to where I could drop him off. I had to be sure that when I dropped him off that it was a safe place and that no harm would come to him.

On my way back to the transfer center, I realized that I go past the police department. Across the street from the police department is the train station. He'd be safe if I dropped him there because there usually are numerous police officers milling around and perhaps if he wanted to, he could catch the train to take him to his home, wherever that might be.

Speaking loud enough for him to hear me, I called my dispatcher and told them that I had a special passenger on board and that I was going to drop him off across the street from the train station. I informed dispatch that I needed to deviate a block or two off my route and needed their permission. My dispatcher OK'd my deviation immediately because they knew exactly where I was headed, the police department. When I was talking to dispatch I exaggerated and overly pronounced that I was going to drop him off across the street from the train station. I did not say the police department. My Dispatcher then asked me if I needed any assistance when I reached my now deviated destination. I told them that I would let them know, but: as for now everything was under control.

I then drove my bus to my now new destination, the police department. I don't think that my lone passenger had a clue as to where we were going. As I pulled up to the front doors of the police department, I got on the internal bus microphone and announced to my lone passenger that this is where he needed to get off the bus.

By his actions I could tell that he knew exactly where we were. He got up from the seat, looked around out the window and hobbled to the front of the bus. He made some comment to himself about all the police officers milling around in the area.

I told him that the train station was across the street and then I causally mentioned that there would be a train leaving for Chicago in a few minutes. Wanting him to know that I had him figured out, I suggested to him that perhaps he should first go to the police department, that's the building right in front of us, and tell the nice man in the blue uniform, at the front desk, where he was trying to go and what he was doing.

As my prefabricating passenger exited the bus, he most graciously thanked me for the bus ride and my generous hospitality. What a phony. I could tell by the look on his face that he was scared as hell because he realized that I caught on to his scam. I'm not sure that the police could have done anything to him because after all; I did pay his bus fare for him. As he was walking down the bus steps, I said to him, "have a nice day guy. Make sure you tell those guys in there that the bus driver sent you."

By now he was off the bus and I was closing the bus doors. I was more than glad to get him off my bus. After he got off the bus and was standing on the side walk that lead to the police department front doors. He stood there for a moment as if he was thinking about what he was going to do next. He glanced back at the bus and then started slowly walking with a pronounced limp toward the police department.

As I was pulling the bus away from the curb and was driving past him he did something that made me laugh. I watched as my new found friend immediately change direction and was now running, as fast as he could toward the train station. I thought of it as a miracle. I also noticed that he had taken his wallet out and had some paper money in his hand. Another miracle performed right before my eyes. I guess that he did have money and was going to pay for his train ticket, I don't know.

I knew then for sure, that this guy thought that he was going to push this small city bumpkin bus driver, me, around. It's a shame that this individual felt that just because I fell for his crying and sore leg gig that I would be ignorant enough to fall for his "heaven is my home routine." His lost, not mine.

More important, I was irked at myself for trusting this guy. I have another motto and that is "Don't mess with somebody smarter that you." Obviously this guy figured out who was the smarter when I dropped him off and gave him the choice between the police department and the train station.

All it cost me was a dollar, which I paid out of my own money for his bus fare, to learn just a little more about ways people will try to rip the bus drivers off. I put that in my memory banks and I'm sure it won't happen again. I told the other bus drivers about the incident and they are all aware of it now. My supervisor had me fill out an incident report, just to have everything documented.

The city that I drive in is located between Chicago and Milwaukee; so we get quit a few incidents like this per year. Hey, if someone falls on hard times, I'll be one of the first in line to do what I can to help. But if I think that if someone is attempting to make me look like a fool, that's another story. I thought about this guy and his scam. What a shame that he went through all those lies just to save him the cost of a bus ride. I hope he realized that everybody not as dumb as he thinks they are.

That was the first and last time I have ever seen that guy. I know that the train that he was catching was headed to Chicago and that was a good place for him. I'm sure that he wouldn't pull that scam on the drivers down there. I've got a pretty good memory and I know that if I ever see this guy again that I will be taken in by his little games.

Even though incidents like this happen; I'm confident that I will not hesitate to do the right thing. And yes, I still carry extra change in my lunch box just incase someone tells me that they need to ride the bus and they don't have any money.

Chapter 11

THE CLAY FIGHT!

A lot of time things would go away if only I had learned to keep my comments to myself. On day I was on a middle school run and the students decide that they were going to have a clay fight with modeling clay that they had taken from the school art room. I did not realize what was going on until I noticed that many of the young adults were laughing hysterically as they exited the bus. Upon closer examination, I noticed that many of the disembarking students had clay smudges on their clothing, face and hands.

I stopped the bus and walked to the rear seat of the bus only to find a wet modeling clay mess. Clay was spread on the seats, windows and floor. The clay was drying and was becoming almost dirt like. I still had a handful of students left on the bus that needed to be dropped off. I wasn't sure if any of them were to blame or involved for the mess or not, so; didn't make an issue with them. I notified my dispatcher that I needed to swap buses because of the mess. I had another school run to perform and there was no way that the high school students would sit down on the messy clay attired seats.

Needless to say I was irritated because I had to drive back to the transit garage. This detour to pick up a replacement bus was about ten minutes out of my scheduled route   Picking up a replacement bus up was going to cause me to be late picking up a group of high school students.

I picked up my replacement bus and went to pick up the high school students. I was a little later that I normally was and told them that I had a problem with my other bus and had to get a replacement. I did not tell the high school kids about the clay fight that the middle school students had had because I figured, why give them any ideas.

The next day when I arrived at the middle school to pick up my clay throwing students, I was ready and on the look out for any traces of clay that the students might be smuggling on the bus. There were about twenty students on the bus when a young lady, who had gotten on earlier, came to the front of the bus and frantically said to me, "Those boys have clay again today. My mom says that if I get all messy again that I would be in big trouble. Could you please do something about it?" I immediately thought to myself; "So much for my watchful eye. Those kids probably could have snuck a hippopotamus on the bus and I would have not noticed. "

"Say no more", I exclaimed. I glanced out the bus window looking for a teacher or bus monitor for assistance. There was a teacher present so I honked the bus horn to get her attention. Kind of a rude way to get her attention, but: it worked. When she looked toward the bus, I motioned for her to come and help me.

I can usually tell a lot about a person the way that they are dressed and this teacher was defiantly the one that I wanted to handle the clay situation. I can remember back when I was in school that there were teachers who you did not want to get on the wrong side of and she defiantly fit that profile. She was conservatively dressed in a pants suit outfit and had her hair pulled back in a ponytail. Around her neck she had a lanyard with a gym whistle, numerous keys and a multitude of key cards. She reminded me of a gym teacher that I once knew. There was no doubt in my mind that she was going to be firm and could handle any situation with the kids.

She walked up to the open front doors of the bus and looked into my eyes and said very pleasantly to me, "Can I help you Sir."

I said, "Yes. It has been reported to me that some of your industrious students took some clay out of the art room and plan on having a clay fight on the bus again. They had a clay fight yesterday and I'm not going to put up with one today. Would you please help me?"

She looked at me and her eyes narrowed. If I recall properly her blue eyes turned from blue to a fiery red and the look on her face went from calm to anger in a matter of seconds. I know that look. That look was real close to the look that my wife gives me when I forget to do what I was told to do or when an argument is imminent. I knew that those kids where in trouble and that she was going to take care of them. Yippee!

She walked up the front steps of the bus with her shoulders back and her head held high. She stopped at the standee line facing the mass of students and said in a very loud confident voice, "May I have your attention please!"

Let me tell you, I've got and internal microphone system on the bus and her voice carried though that bus better than that microphone and speaker system could have. She put her hands on her hips and thrusted her chest out waiting for the students on the bus to quite down and give her their utmost and undivided attention.

Mean while I just sat there in the drivers seat gloating and watching a master at work. She was standing about two feet away from me and was dead serious about the situation at hand. When all the students on the bus had stopped in their tracks and were giving her their undivided attention; she seriously said, "All right who has clay balls?" In which I instinctively muttered under my breathe, "Gumby."

As soon as I said that it dawned on me that I messed up. The young teacher, still standing facing the students with her hands on her hips snapped her head toward me and gave me a glare that scared me. I immediately turned toward the front of the bus and put both hands on the bus steering wheel. I assumed a non-aggressive position. This was the closest that I could get to the fetal position without actually getting on the floor and curling up. I was hoping that she would see my demeanor as submissive. I guess I did that to show her that I knew that I messed up and just wanted her to leave me alone.

Her head snapped back toward the students and she started making her way toward the rear of the bus. It reminded me of Moses spreading the Red Sea. As she walked through the mass of young adults, they were getting out of her way as to not become the affection or center of her attention. I sat there wondering if I should get up and help, but; almost immediately I came to my senses and said, "no way."

A minute or so passed, it seemed like forever, and she came walking back through the multitude of students with two young male students in tow. I felt sorry for them, but; a little sorry for myself because they knew that I was the one who told on them. I said to myself," Whatever."

As the young teacher and her two enterprising students got to the front of the bus near the standee line she looked at the boys and said, "Do you two have anything to say to the nice Bus Driver?" These two kids about now were thinking that I was anything but nice for squealing on them. I sat there and looked them in the eye. I could smell the fear that they had of this teacher. I figured, better them than me.

They both replied immediately and in unison, "We're sorry about the clay mess, do you want us to clean it up?" I said that I would contact my dispatcher and let them decide. I didn't want to make any decisions that I would later regret. I felt that I was in enough hot water now. While I was waiting for my dispatcher to respond the young teacher was being very apologetic to me. She was telling me about school pride and how the new vandalism policy was going to be applied here. I said to myself, "whatever." I was scared of her anyways and I just wanted to continue with my route. I kept thanking her for her help and kept repeating, "Kids will be kids."

I informed dispatch of the situation and asked about whether or not dispatch wanted the two young adults to come to the transit garage and clean some buses as a punishment. This wasn't my call and I didn't care one way or another. As I was carrying on my conversation on with my dispatcher, the teacher and the two apologetic students stood patiently by waiting for an answer. All the other passengers on the bus remained quite and waited to see what would happen next. There were quit a few kids on the bus, but; nobody on the bus was saying a word about anything. All the kids on the bus obviously knew that this teacher meant business.

My dispatcher told me to relay a message to the teacher and kids. The message was that if they promised not to do anything like that again that the transit department would clean up their mess this time. I turned to the teacher and kids and repeated to them word for word what my dispatcher had said. I spoke slowly and calmly so not to give any misinterpretations. Both the kids immediately promised that nothing like this would happen again. I'm sure that they were scared and meant what they said. The young teacher nodded her head in agreement. I relayed their responses back to dispatch and told her that I was going to continue with my route.

The young teacher apologized again and then led the students off the bus. As they were disembarking the bus she turned to me and said, "We have to go see the art instructor now."

I thought for sure that she was going to make a comment about my "Gumby" remark.

A couple days had passed before I was scheduled to run that particular school run again because of scheduling conflicts. When I was scheduled to do that route I was a little apprehensive, but; I figure everything was over and everything was forgotten.

As the students started to board the bus, I recognized one of the students as the young lady who had approached me about the boys and the impending clay fight a few days earlier. I remembered her because she was the one who had told me about her mom getting mad if she came home from school again with clay on her clothes. I tried to ignore her as best as I could. As she started up the front bus steps of the bus, she stopped dead in her tracks when she saw that it was me driving the bus. She stood there for a second or two and then turned around and got off the bus. I don't know why, but; I had the impression that she somehow had gotten into trouble over the clay incident. I watched as she walked away from the bus obviously looking for somebody. I was checking the other student's bus passes and keeping an eye on her to see what she was up to.

What happened next surprised me. The little snitch ran up to the teacher on bus duty, said something to her. When she did that they both turned toward me and started walking toward the bus. I'm not paranoid, but; I was trying to figure out what I had done wrong and why were these people coming over to obviously confront me about something.

As they got closer I noticed that the teacher was in fact the teacher that had handled the clay incident. My first thought was "Oh no! She took care of those boys and now it's my turn."

I had no place to run and I couldn't just drive away, so I just sat there cowering behind the steering wheel. All the students had gotten on the bus by now and were engaged in small talk. They were being orderly and quiet. The young lady and the teacher got on the bus and the young lady went to join the other students at the rear of the bus.

Obviously I was being set up. That left me alone at the front of the bus with the teacher. I was wondering what she wanted, but; I knew that she wanted to talk about my Gumby comment.

I sat there waiting to get yelled at as the young teacher moved closer toward me. I was quivering and wanted to run. The teacher stopped about one foot away from me and leaned over and quietly whispered to me, "You had good timing on that comment that you made to me about 'Gumby' and you did it very discretely. I thank you for that, but: it's a good thing that those boys weren't playing with steel balls, right?"

I looked at her and realize that she too had a good sense of humor. We both had a good laugh and I told her that I would watch my comments. Every time I saw that teacher throughout the school year I had to chuckle. I'm sure that she did the same. I learned two things that day. The first was to keep a look out for clay and the second was to keep my comments to myself. The first one is easy the second one, well; I'm still working on it.

Chapter 12

THERE ARE NO RATS AND IT DOESN'T STINK

I've heard the expression "From the mouth of babe's" numerous times and never really understood what it meant until I experienced something first handed. I get along really well with most of the kids that ride my bus. I think that it's because I treat them with respect and they know that I do it sincerely. They know what they can and can't do on my bus. I don't allow the "N'" word, no swearing and no bullying are rules that they know that I am serious about.

If a kid is going to school and is a couple pennies short of bus fare or have no fare, I let them ride with what they have. I pay their fare for them with my own money. It cost me a couple bucks each week, but; it's my way of giving back to the community. I keep a running track of what they owe and make the difference up myself. I don't tell them that I do this. The only stipulation that I give is that they can ride the bus if they promise to stay in school and not cause any trouble that day.

Many of the kids that ride my bus come from broken families. I know this because most of the time, they tell me. Occasionally, I guess out of pride, some of the kids won't say a word about anything concerning their families. I can usually tell who these individuals are and try to respect their privacy. I figure why make it tougher on them. I always mention to the kids if they have a problem and want to talk about, well here I am. I treat them all the same regardless of who they are. Quit a few of the kids, or young adults as I call them, take me up on my offer and you'd be surprised at what they tell me. Maybe, through my actions, I can give them a little self esteem and self confidence by showing them that respect demands respect. Quit a few of the kids call me "Uncle Marty."

One young lad, about thirteen or fourteen years of age, got on my bus one day and was really excited. I knew that he had come from a broken home because he told me all about it. I was someone he could talk to because he knew that I wouldn't tell anyone. I could tell, by his actions, that he wanted to tell me something important.

Now this kid is what I consider a tough kid. He is not a bully, but: he can take care of himself. I've seen this kid help other kids. He has helped others carry their books, chase lost papers in the wind and tell other kids that were bulling others to knock it off because the kid that they were picking on was his friend. Only to find out that he never knew the kid that was being picked on he just didn't like it. He just didn't want anybody to get in trouble. He had a heart of gold, but he also had a tough image to uphold. Many times he would ask other kids that were screaming on the bus to knock it off because it bothered the bus driver. I appreciated him for doing that.

This morning, he was my only passenger on the bus. This was because he had walked about four blocks away from his normal bus stop to meet me at the end of the bus line. I greeted him as he boarded and he just stood there by the fare box smiling.

Knowing that he had something on his mind, I said, "OK, what's up?"

He then proceeded to tell me that his mother had found a different place for them to live and that they were moving. He was really excited. The only bad thing was that he would not be taking the bus to school any more because his new school was only a block away from his new house. His mom said that she had no problem if he and his brother walked to school. I was happy for him because he was happy. I shook his hand and congratulated him.

Many times the young adults will get on my bus and tell me stories, but; I knew that he was serious and he was looking forward to the move. A few weeks went by and my young friend had stopped riding the bus. I saw him and his brother walking to school a few times and they waved at me. I figured that they had moved into their new house and he and his family were starting a new chapter in their lives, I was happy for him and his family and I wished them the best. I did miss him riding the bus because he was such a pleasant young man and we had many serious conversations.

One day, about a month after he stopped riding the bus, I encountered my young friend at the end of the bus line. He had gone out of his way to get on my bus. I knew that he wanted to talk to me about something. He knew by catching me at the end of the line that he would be the only rider on the bus for at least three or four blocks. I was happy to see him and asked how he and his family were doing. He told me that his family really liked their new house.

I asked him how he liked it. He gave me a serious look and said to me, "Uncle Marty, I really like my new house a lot. Do you know what I like best about it?"

I said, "No, what's that?" I was figuring he would say something about being close to school or something of that nature. Perhaps he was excited because he and his brother got their own bedrooms. I curiously waited for his reply.

He said, "I really like the basement of our new house."

I didn't know what to make of it. I immediately thought that maybe the basement was finished or perhaps he and his brother had a game room. I didn't know.

What he said next almost knocked me over. He said, "It has a dirt floor and crumbling walls, but; there are no rats and it doesn't stink like all our other houses did. I was humbled by his words. He continued, "mom says that I can go down in our new basement, if I want, and just think and be alone or read a book if I want to." It's really a good place to get a way from it all."

I knew this kid had class. I was thinking inside the box again and not facing reality. This kid and his family were experiencing something that many of us take for granted and that is a nice clean house and a safe environment.

My friend got off the bus and said that he'd keep in touch with me. It's now been quite a while since I've seen that young man. I really hope that everything is going good. I think about how selfish we all are when it comes to things like that. It seems that we all either ignore or avoid conversations like he and I had that day. Now every time I hear "From the mouth of Babe's", I think of my young friend and how fortunate I truly am. That phrase has given me a new perspective on how I judge others or should I say on how I try not to judge others.

Chapter 13

You're a penny Shy. I won't move the bus!!

I get a chance to meet a lot of people on the bus and hear all kinds of stories. After the recent hurricanes destroyed many of the homes and businesses on our countries southern coast, I had the privilege and opportunity to meet many of the hurricane aftermath victims. Each one of them had a different story, but; they were all the same. There were at least twenty different people with whom I spoke to about their plight. They all came from different cities and states, but; were affected one way or another by the different storms. I was told accounts of how people lost their homes, possessions and love ones. Each one touched me in a way that I hope that I never forget.

I know that some individuals would prefabricate and try to take advantage of the situation, just to make a fast buck. I'm very confident that all the hurricane refugees that I encountered were genuine and making the best out of a bad situation.

Most of the hurricane refugees that I met told me horror stories of being bounced around the country from shelter to shelter. After being displaced by the storms, they were moved from motel to shelter and from city to city.

It seems that most of the southern shelters and motels were filled quickly, so federal agencies sent the masses further north with promises of housing and employment opportunities. There were tent cities in the south, but; they filled up fast with the storm refugees. Also many of the tent cities had to be disassembled whenever a new storm depression threatened the area

It was the holiday season and winter and I just couldn't understand how these people kept their sanity and sense of humor in such trying times. Among the many things that the hurricane victims told me were that most of their belonging were salvageable, but; had to be left behind because they was no room in the shelters for personal items. The only things that they could bring to the shelter were clothing, personal hygiene items and any small items that they could carry. No pets were allowed in the shelters.

I was told how they packed as many pictures, documents and personal items that they could carry in suitcases, but; most of their valuable family treasures had to be abandoned and left behind to be picked up later. When the storm victims had returned to their houses to retrieve and salvage personal items, with the authorities' permission, many of the victims found that their homes had been looted and most of saleable items were now gone.

Many were forced to leave immediately and didn't have time to reinforced damaged areas of their homes. When they did return days later, the winds and rains had taken its toll on their belongings and nothing was left but rubble.

I met a family that lost all their personal items to the storms. Through it all, the storms could not take away this family's dignity, courage and determination. This displaced family that I met told me many personal things and confined in me. They weren't trying to con me or use me. I was touched when they referred to me, as they put it, a pillar of strength for them.

My befriended family included: the Dad, the mom and a daughter. This family used to have a normal life, but; that was all changed because of the hurricane. I don't remember which hurricane it was that displaced them, but; that doesn't really matter anyhow. When times were normal for this family, the mom ran a day care out of her house and was a certified licensed practical nurse. Her husband worked for a swimming pool cleaning service and at night he was working on an accountant degree at the local community college. The couple's teenaged daughter was an honor student and was enthusiastically involved in high school sports. She told me that she was twice an all conference point guard and that she was just a junior.

They said that they had a couple hundred dollars, but; the way things were going that it would be gone in a short time. The wife showed me a debit card that they had gotten from the government. She said that it was their only lifeline that they had left because they didn't know when the insurance company was going to settle with them. I didn't ask how much money it was worth because, quite frankly, it was none of my business She kept telling me how thankful she was that she had kept flood insurance on their property and belongings even though her husband had thought she dropped it years ago.

The husband told me that they did qualified for government sponsored lodging and employment benefits, but; they didn't know when they would start or how long they would last. He also said that the family was scheduled to move into a house in another city in a few weeks, but; they weren't given any more information about it. That time frame for this incidentally was aright around Christmas day. All they were told was to hang in there and somebody will notify them when it's their turn. They did say that they had to leave a phone number with some agency incase they needed to be contacted.

I have many fond memories of this family even though I spent a short time with them. One of the memories of this family included a horror story of how this family was treated on a city transit bus, in my city, by an insensitive bus driver. I am usually quick to point out when my passengers don't use common sense, but; in this case it was the bus driver who was the culprit.

It was mid December and winter in Wisconsin and this family had never before experienced snow. They were living in a government sponsored motel and the clothes on their back had been donated to them by the Salvation Army. Not being accustoms to the cold weather; no matter what they did or how they tried, they couldn't keep warm. They had new boots and gloves, something that they weren't used to wearing. We that were raised in areas where it snows know that when you have a large pair of gloves or mittens on; that you tend to be very clumsy and your dexterity skills of your hands diminish to almost nothing. You think that something like that would be common knowledge, but it obviously isn't.

Hey, I'm Marty. I drive the bus

The following incident was reported to me by the family that I mentioned and no less than seven different regular bus riders from my route. This happened on my day off. These passengers are people who work at the local hotels and strip mall out near the end of my route. They had no reason to make up any stories and were appalled as I was, when I was told of the incident that they all witnessed.

One day while the family, my friends, was waiting for the bus; the husband did not realize the problems that can arise when you are wearing mittens. The husband held his bus fare, which is one dollar, in his mitten covered hand. He held the coins on the outside of the mitten and not in his covered palm of his hand. He told me that he had one dollar in change and that change included five pennies. His wife and daughter each had bus tokens and were holding them in their bare, uncovered hands.

The bus pulled up to the curb to pick them up and the wife and daughter got on the bus. They put their tokens into the fare box and went and sat down in a seat. As the husband started up the front steps of the bus he lost his footing and fell into the freshly fallen snow. When he fell in the snow, the change that he was holding in his mitten covered hand, fell from his mitten and into the freshly fallen snow. I was told that he got up and brushed himself off. He then immediately started looking frantically for the coins in the snow. Meanwhile the bus driver started yelling at him to hurry up because she had a schedule to keep. He said that at first he thought that she was joking with him because she had witnessed him fall in the snow. But as it turned out, she was being obnoxious and sarcastic.

The man picked up his change from the snow got on the bus. He wiped the snow off the coins and hastily counted them. He then put the coins into the fare-box. He then turned toward and started to walk to the rear of the bus to sit down by his wife and daughter. He told me that he was smiling and laughing as he walked toward his wife and daughter because earlier they were joking between themselves of which one of them would fall into the snow first. Obviously he lost.

As he was walking to join his family, that was when the bus driver yelled at him to come back to the front of the bus because he did not put enough money into the fare-box. She was talking loud enough so that every body on the bus could hear her. The man turned around and walked up to the bus driver and said, "That he put all the money that he had in the fare box." As it turns out he had just put ninety nine cents in the fare box and not the one dollar adult fare. He was one penny shy of a full fare. Technically, he did not pay his fare.

The bus driver, waiting for a penny, told the man that she was not going to move the bus until he paid his entire fare. The man then got off the bus and starting frantically looking in the snow for the one penny that he had lost. Meanwhile the man's wife, wondering why her husband had gotten off the bus, came to the front of the bus and approached the driver. She then asked the bus driver, "What the problem was?"

The bus driver snapped back at her and said, "This bus ain't moving until he pays the entire fare. The bus doesn't run on excuses." The man's wife then asked the bus driver, "How much more does he owe?"

The bus driver rudely exclaimed, "One penny. He just put ninety nine cents in I'm not moving this bus until he pays the full adult fare, just like everybody else. I'm sick and tired of you people trying to rip everyone off."

The wife looked at the bus driver and said, "Are you being serious?" To which the bus driver screamed, "Your damn straight I am. I'm not moving this bus until I get that penny!"

Meanwhile, the husband is looking in the snow-bank for the lost penny; the wife is looking through her purse for change and the daughter is checking her coat pockets. They were all searching for one penny. Now remember, this family a couple weeks back had just lost everything that they owned and now are being harassed and chastised for one penny.

The wife told me that after a few minutes of looking for a penny; that she started to laugh. She did have a five dollar bill and was going to put that in the fare-box; just to put an end to what was happening. She said that she couldn't believe what was going on. She said about that time was when the bus driver then gave her a friendly suggestion. The bus driver said, "Why don't you borrow a penny from one of the other passengers."

At that, at least seven different passengers, who witnessed the whole ordeal and didn't know this family, got up and offered the family the missing penny. A young man, who always rides the bus to work everyday acted first. He put his magazine that he was reading down and got up from his seat; he walked up to the crowd of passengers that was now gathered near the fare box and reached around them and put a quarter in the fare-box. He then turned around and went back to his seat. As he turned and walked back to his seat past the other passengers and driver he sarcastically said, "What a joke."

The bus driver, still not happy about the situation, told the man to get on the bus or she would leave him there. She also told the wife and daughter to sit down and quit bothering the other passengers.

The bus driver then made another sarcastic remark to herself, but was now satisfied the entire fare had been paid. She told everybody on the bus to sit down; she closed the bus doors and pulled away from the curb to continue the route. When she pulled away from the curb, a few of the passengers had not made it back to their seats and almost fell from the buses acceleration. One passenger told the driver that she should have waited until everybody was seated until she took off. The drivers response was, "You don't like my driving; next time walk!"

The man and his family were very gracious for the response from the other passengers. The man's wife was also obviously embarrassed about the entire incident. She thanked the male passenger for the quarter and said that she would give him his quarter back when they get downtown by the bank, or; if he preferred, she would mail a quarter to him. The young man told the lady to forget about it went back to reading his magazine. She was touched by his actions and she said that she started to cry.

The passengers that witnessed the actions of the bus driver approached me at different times when I returned to work the next day. They said that they couldn't believe what was going on. They said that couldn't figure out why the bus driver was acting like she was. All the passengers knew that the driver in question was a replacement driver for me because it was my day off. All the passengers that were on the bus were shocked at the driver's actions and confused by them. It made me feel good when the passengers said, "that they would rather have me than her drive the bus."

I told the passengers that they needed to call the city transit department with their concerns. Most of their responses to that were, "we called on issues before and nothing got done. I'm not going to waste my time." I said to them, "did you call on me? Did I do something wrong?" They all assured me that it was another issue that they were experiencing with a different driver.

This incident was told to me the next day by that family and confirmed by none less than seven other people that were on the bus at the time. The passengers knew that by telling me of the incident that I would tell my superiors so that something like this would not happen again. When the family told me of what had transpired I was ashamed. I was ashamed that they were treated the way they were.

I spoke to my superiors and dispatcher when I got back to the garage that evening. I was mad as I relayed to them what I had been told, but: I was more ashamed of my fellow driver's actions. My superiors said that there was nothing that they could do about the incident and that there was no disciplinary action required because the driver was doing her job. This was the typical response from my superiors when they don't want to admit one of their driver buddies were wrong.

My dispatcher was livid after I told the story to her. She told me to stop by the dispatcher's desk the next day before I start my route because she would leave an envelope for me to give to the family. I asked what was going to be in the envelope and she told me that she was going to give the family some complimentary passes for their inconveniences. She also said that she was going to talk to the route supervisor about the other driver's actions because this wasn't the first time something like this had happened.

The next day before I started my route, I picked up the envelope that the dispatcher had told me about the night before. When I saw the family later that day, I gave the envelope to them and expressed how sorry and embarrassed I was. I told them that my dispatcher had taken the extra step to help them and had gotten them some bus passes. I relayed to the family that she too, was truly sorry for the incident. I told the family not to judge all of our cities bus drivers by the actions of a few. They said that they understood and thanked me graciously for what I had done to help. They asked for a phone number where they could reach my dispatcher so that they could also thank them. I gave them the dispatcher first name and told the family to just call the city transit department and they would get a hold of her.

I occasionally saw the family for the next week or two after that incident. Christmas was still a couple days away. But; their spirit and attitude amazed me. I tried not to talk about the holidays when they were on the bus because I knew that their holiday was going to be a sad one for them.

The day before Christmas I picked the family up at the bus stop by their motel. They were all acting very happy and excited about something and I didn't know what. That's when they told me that a man from some government agency had contacted them and that they were next on the list for housing. I thought to myself, "What a great Christmas gift for them." They spoke of how things were looking up for them and how life was going to get back to some what normal.

My wife and I gave the family a Christmas envelope with a couple bucks in it. It wasn't much, but; the family knew that the gift was straight from our hearts and they truly appreciated it.

They said that if they didn't see me again that they would always remember my kindness.

Well, as it turns out, I have never seen that family again. I can only hope that things are working out for them and their life is getting back to somewhat normal. They are a strong family with good values and I'm sure that their doing well. Sometime when I'm driving the bus and pass the bus stop where I met them, I think about them.

Its amazing how people, that you really don't know, can affect your life. I could only hope that if my works do get published one day, that some of my southern displaced friends would read my book and contact me so that I could see them again. But then again, what do I know, I just drive the bus.

Chapter 14

My baby ate the bus transfer!!

A lot of people are always trying to get free bus rides. It is usually the same ones over and over again. The excuses and stories that we bus drivers hear about lost change, missing bus passes and misplaced transfers go on and on. The stories and excuses that we are told, differ from day to day. The bottom line is; that people want to ride the bus for free.

We bus drivers can be quit skeptical and are usually on top of most situations We are typically aware of instances and circumstances that are being applied by individuals trying to take the opportunity to rip the transit system off. That's our job: public transportation. This of course means that we drivers are responsible to see that everybody pays the established posted bus fare. That payment can come in the form of cash or a bus pass, either one is acceptable by me. What's good for one; is good for everybody.

Of course common sense comes into play here too. For instance, let's consider the bus driver that encounters the same person everyday of the week for the past two years and that individual produces a valid bus pass on each of those days. Then, one day that person gets on the bus and tells the bus driver that they forgot their purse or wallet at home and that they don't have their bus pass with them. The individual then ask the bus driver if they could ride the bus that day and show the bus driver their bus pass tomorrow.

The bus driver now has a dilemma; should they charge that individual a full fare, or; should the bus driver let the person ride the bus, knowing full well, that the individual will show the bus pass to the bus driver the next day. Everybody might think that this is a no brainier, but; it's up to the bus driver what he wants the individual to do

A situation like this can actually go either way. This is where you would think common sense should be applied, but a lot of times it isn't. Believe it or not, there are bus drivers who are unable to think for themselves. These are the drivers that interpret the established rules in black and white and follow them to the letter. This is not a win/win situation, but rather; a lose/lose situation. What happens in cases like this is; the passenger gets mad at the bus driver for doing their job and the bus driver gets frustrated with the passenger for not understanding their position.

One day a lady got on my bus with a toddler in a stroller and told me that the baby had eaten her bus transfer. I've heard a lot of excuses about lost transfers, but; this was one excuse that I haven't heard before. I said to the lady, "You'll have to show me a valid bus transfer or you'll have to pay an adult fare." I wasn't trying to be mean or disrespectful to the lady; I was just trying to do my job. By the ladies reaction, I could tell that she was upset with me. She stood there for a few seconds looking at me as if she were wondering what to do. Then very sarcastically she said, "I'll show you my transfer."

For security reason our transit system changes ink colors of our bus transfers daily. The bus transfers are hand punched by the bus drivers. The punched transfers are specified by color, date, route and time. This is done to prevent passengers from using expired transfers and short changing the transit system of funds.

I sat in the driver's seat watching and waiting to see what she was going to do next. The lady then turned toward the toddler that she had in the stroller. Without warning or saying a word to the toddler; she put her index finger and thumb into the toddler's mouth. She then started moving her finger and thumb around in the toddler's mouth in a sweeping motion as if she was searching for something. After she had found what she was searching for, she pulled her finger and thumb out of the toddler's mouth. The toddler started to cry. The lady was now holding what appeared to be a chewed, wet, balled up, wad of paper. She then unraveled the wet, wadded ball the best that she could and she held it up for me to see.

The toddler was now screaming and crying, obviously wanting to chew on the paper. The lady ignored his pleas. I was surprised at what she was holding. Sure enough, she didn't lie. The toddler was chewing on her bus transfer, like she had told me, as if it were gum or candy. This Gooey mess that she was proudly displaying to me was defiantly a bus transfer of the right daily color. I couldn't see if the punches were valid because of it being chewed. I figured that if she had gone through that much trouble to get it out of the toddler's mouth, it had to be a valid transfer.

After I acknowledged to her, that I thought that it was indeed a valid transfer, the lady turned back toward the stroller. She then bent over toward the toddler and inserted the wet colored wad of paper back into the crying toddler's mouth. I informed her that that transfer was good for one hour from the time that when it was issued and that I was not going to give her another one.

By now the lady was walking toward the rear of the bus pushing her stroller. While she was looking for a vacant seat; she told me that she understood and that this would never happen again. The toddler had stopped crying now and was contently chewing on the wad of paper. As I closed the bus doors and continued with my route, I wondered how many times that day did that lady show that chewed up wad of paper to the other bus drivers. I put that experience in the back of my mind for future reference. All I know is that the next time a passenger tells me that their baby ate their transfer; I can tell them that I still need to see it. Not that I'm going to take it, but: I still need to see it.

Chapter 15

SO YOU KIDS WANT TO PLAY, HUH!!

On school runs in the morning it would be safe to say that the student passengers are in no hurry to get to school. They haven't a care in the world because they know that the bus driver will get them to school on time. If the bus is late getting them to school; the kids don't care because they have someone to blame and that is the bus driver. When the kids are going home, it's a different story. They all have an agenda, regardless of what it may be, and they go ballistic if they have to deviate from that agenda. I guess that they figure that since they spent all day in school, this free time is owed to them as a reward.

The students on my last afternoon school run, a while back, found out that the bus driver can play games too. The bus was packed and some of the young adults thought that it would be funny to play with the chime line. The chime line is the cord that the passengers pull to alert the driver that they want off at the next stop. When the kids pulled the chime line, I would stop at the next stop and no one would get off the bus. Since the bus was jammed with kids I had to make sure no one wanted off and that the back door was clear before I closed it. I could hear many of the students laughing. When I looked in the rearview interior mirror many of them just sat there making remarks about how nobody wanted to get off. I got on the internal microphone and requested that they not pull the cord unless they wanted off the bus. After my second warning they continued to play with the cord. I turned the internal microphone back on and announced that I was turning the chime off and it was my turn to play. Many of the young passengers made sarcastic remarks such as, "Ooh were scared." And my favorite, "What are you going do?"

I called my dispatcher and informed them that I was going to be running a little late because the kids on my bus wanted to play. I also reminded Dispatch that this was my last run of the day so adult passengers were not going to be inconvenienced. The dispatcher asked me if I needed any assistance and I said no.

Well I thought to myself, "Let the games begin." What I proceeded to do was stop at every corner along the scheduled route and open the front and back door. After the doors were opened I announced over the internal microphone,"The bus has been stopped, if you are disembarking please watch your step and have a nice day". All the kids on the bus thought that this was hysterical. They were laughing and carrying on about how the bus driver was acting like a fool. I continued to do my stops and my announcement for the next five or six corners.

Many of the kids started to become irritated and started making comments like," Come on man, I want to get home."

And being the professional driver that I am, I explained to them that I was sorry, but: I needed to stop at every corner because by their playing with the chime line, I didn't want anybody to miss their stop. So the only way I could make sure was to stop at every corner. Now all he kids on the bus were starting to complain every time I stopped and gave my little announcement.

The next three stops were very interesting because some of the playful students decided that they could walk faster than the bus was driving, so they tried. I guess they now realize that the bus is a mechanical device and doesn't get winded from lack of oxygen like students do.

The next stop that I came to was one that one of the playful instigators got off so I figured to miss that corner and stop at the third one down. When I past up his stop his was yelling, "Stop the bus, this is my stop!" My replied was, "Please be seated until the bus comes to a complete stop." He just sat down and was saying things under his breath. When I pulled up and stopped three blocks from his bus stop things just weren't as funny as they were a few minutes earlier. At his new bus stop I opened only the front door of the bus and requested that passengers please exit through the front door. He came walking to the front of the bus with an angry look on his face. As he was getting off the bus I said, "Do you want to do the same thing tomorrow, I thought that this was fun." He didn't say a word and got off the bus.

I felt that the other students that were on the bus had enough of my fun and that I got my point across. All the laughing and jubilation had been replaced with silence. I announced that I was turning the chime line back on and would continue the route in a normal manner, only if they wanted me to. Out of the thirty or so students that were on the bus perhaps only two did not respond with a resounding "YES."

As I pulled up to bus-stops and dropped my passengers off, many of the students used the front bus door to exit. As they would walk past me they would apologize and tell me that they were sorry for their childish behavior. A few of the students stood there after they apologized. I think that they were waiting for an apology from me. That sure wasn't going to happen. Hey, they started it and I finished it.

I finished my route about ten minutes later than I normally do. When I turned my paperwork in my dispatcher asked me if there was anything that they needed to know. I thought about it for about thirty seconds and said "No. I did have a situation on the bus but I took care of it."

As fate would have it, the very next day, I was given the same routes that I had the day before. This included my school run and my chime ringing students. I got to the school early and debated with myself about whether or not to mess with the kids, but; I figured that they had learned their lesson. And besides, I'm the grownup and they are the kids. School was dismissed and one by one the students started to get on the bus. Most of the students that were getting on the bus remembered me from the day before and either said, "Hi" to me or hurried to the rear of the bus and whispered to their friends. I'm sure that they were talking about yesterdays bus ride home. I figured that we'll just see how the bus ride today turns out.

When all the students were on the bus and it was time to leave I started to pull out of the bus stop. The students were all anxious to get home. The students were being quiet and things appeared to be going normally, until someone pulled the chime line as a joke. The bus went silent.

I glanced into the interior rearview mirror and saw about fifteen children looking at me. Another five or six were talking to a young man that obviously was the one who wanted to play with the chime line. One young lady, who was on the bus for yesterday's ride home, spoke up and worriedly said, "Someone pulled the cord by accident sir. I can assure you that it won't happen again."

I replied, "Well, as long it was an accident and it doesn't happen again there won't be any problems."

The bus was basically quite except for some students who were carrying on with their conversations. The girl who spoke up was talking to the boy, whom I believe, pulled the chime cord. Some of the other students that were sitting by the young man were making little comments to him about yesterdays bus ride home. I felt that the students had everything in control and that the chime pulling pranks were through.

The bus ride that day went normal with the only exception being, ever time a student pulled the chime line the remaining students on the bus would look up toward the front of the bus to see how the bus driver was going to react. After a while it got funny and the kids were making little comments when other students pulled the cord. Since that day, I've never had a problem with students from that school playing with the chime line.

Chapter 16

Appling make-up on a moving bus!!

It's truly remarkable and amazing of what some of these students are capable of doing. For instance, some of the young women have mastered the chore of applying their makeup while riding on a bus. I've told many of them that they should consider employment as bomb technicians because they have such steady nerves and hands.

I don't know what half the makeup is for, but; I'm sure that putting a sharp pencil like object near your eye while riding on a moving bus isn't the brightest thing to do. Some of the young women after they apply their makeup on the bus look as if they had it done at a salon or professionally.

Others aren't as skilled. I'm not going to criticize nor am I going to judge because I know that they are applying the make up to make themselves pretty and presentable. A couple things that I do know are that the rousgh, the red powdery stuff for the cheeks, is supposed to go on the cheeks not on their chin and forehead. The same goes with colored blushes and foundation stuff. Presumably it is supposed to be applied to the face which includes ones cheeks, chin, forehead and nose. I've seen young girls have blush and paste on their blouses and in their hair. I'm really sure that those areas were not their intended targets areas.

You ain't seen nothing until you see how lipstick turns out when it is applied on a moving bus. All I know is that lip stick is supposed to go on the lips. Some of these young girls have lipstick lines that extend to the middle of their cheeks. Some of the lipstick lines are straight and narrow while in other places the lines are crooked and wide. I've also seen lipstick smudged on the tips and sides of their young noses. I feel that I should say something, but; out of fear of offending them I don't. I really think it's supposed to be one way or the other and not a combination of both, but; what do I know I'm just a bus driver.

Have you ever seen one of those horror movies where the evil villain's kind of look like a mutant clown. That is what some of these young makeup appliers remind me of.

Now a day's girls aren't the only ones that wear make up. Young men wear it, but; I've never seen the guys try to apply makeup while riding the bus. Maybe they feel that it's something that should be done at home or their not as adventurous as the young ladies. I don't know.

It was raining one day and I picked up a young man that had mascara around his eyes. I again must say that I really don't know a lot about this stuff either but I've seen television commercials that advertise waterproof mascara. This young lad got on the bus dressed up in all black with numerous silver like chains hanging from his clothes. It wasn't his clothes or the chains that made him stand out, but; rather it was the wet, black makeup dripping down his face. I don't know if mascara is supposed to go on the eyebrows or eyelids or whatever. All I do know is that I needed to make a comment to him.

I've seen this kid before on the bus and he and I had brief conversations so he knows that I don't judge people by what they wear. I asked him how thing were going and he said, "Fine, except for the stupid rain."

I then said to him, "You know that I usually mind my own business and don't have a problem with you, right?"

He immediately said, "Yea, your tight" He then stood there looking at me with his makeup running down his face. Instinctively he wiped his face with his sleeve and in doing so smeared the black makeup even more. Not wanting to belittle or embarrass him I said, "Please look in the mirror." He leaned over and looked up into my interior rearview mirror. When he saw how his make up or mascara was running he immediately took out a white handkerchief and started to wipe the makeup off his face. This is the part of the story that reminds me of a television commercial.

I said to him, "Maybe you should consider getting some waterproof makeup."

He looked quizzically at me and said, "They make makeup that is waterproof?"

I replied, "Hey dude, I don't know much about stuff like that. Maybe you should ask your mom or sister what the best stuff."

He finished wiping his face off as he gazed into the mirror and put his now black hanky in one of his half dozen or so pants pockets. He then turned to go to the rear of the bus to sit down. As he was walking toward the rear of the bus, he stopped and turned toward me and said, "Thanks for telling me about that. I'm going to talk to my mom about what makeup I should and should not use."

I said, "No problem."

I think about that conversation and I just find it hard to believe that a young man and I were talking about makeup. I see that kid every once in awhile and he still is expressing himself by dressing in black and wearing silver chains. I think it's called "Gothic or whatever." One thing I did notice was that he must have had a conversation with someone about makeup. Perhaps they also gave him lessons or two on what and how to apply it. He did go out of his way, not to long after our conversation, to stop and talk to me and show me his updated look. It was raining that day and his makeup was intact. I myself can't figure stuff like that out, but; then again I remember that I used to have long hair and like loud rock music.

Chapter 17

It's OK I don't have germs!!

We bus drivers are usually on the bus for eight plus hours per day so we bring our lunches and drinks with us. I know that there are signs on the bus that say "No eating on the bus," but; all the bus drivers need to get a suck or two on their beverage whenever they get a chance. Sometimes that chance comes when you're waiting for someone to get on or off the bus, but; most of the time it happens when were driving. Now we don't eat a sandwich while were driving for safety reasons, but: we do suck on our soda or water when we get the chance. As much as we would like to go into a fast-food restaurant and sit down and enjoy a meal, it just isn't possible. I bring some snacks and a sandwich which last me all day. The reason for that is the only time I can eat is when I'm at the end of my routes or waiting for transfers. For drinks I bring a bottle of water.

All the bus drivers know of places along each route where they can get their coffee cup filled with either coffee or soda. These little "pit stops" as we call them also gives us a chance to use the comfort stations.

A lot of our more frequent passengers act as if the bus drivers are more like their family than strangers. They tell us about their daily problems and heaven forbid their medical histories. One lady who rides my bus takes medicine at all times of the day. She is an elderly women and told me what each and every one of her pills do and how often she need to take them. Like I say I get more information then I need to know.

This lady is a real sweetheart and means well. She has never been aggressive nor has she ever caused any real problems. She does have some major medical problems and she is dealing with them.

One day while she was a passenger on my bus she told me that she needed to take some of her medicine. I replied back to her that she has to do what she has to do. At that she got up from her seat, walked to the front of the bus, picked up my water bottle from my lunch box and proceeded to drink my water from my bottle. I was waiting at the stoplight and watching traffic and didn't have time to react. She stood there about two feet from me chugging and slurping on my precious water bottle. I watched as she puts her lips and tongue on and in my only water that I had available for the next hour or so. Needless to say I was mad.

When she finished quenching her thirst, she put the cover back on the bottle. I then watched as she put the almost empty water bottle back in my lunch box. She turned and started to walk toward the rear of the bus to sit in the bus seat where she had been sitting. As she was walking she said very loudly, "I ain't got no germs. I needed that drink to wash down that darn pill down."

I wanted to say something, but: my mom always told me if you can't say something nice, keep your mouth shut. So I did.

The elderly women kept talking of how good and refreshing that water was. I said,"Yea I know, that water was a cherry flavored water that I buy special. It cost a little more but I like it"

At that she looked at me and said, "I'm allergic to cherries."

She then asked if she could look at the water bottle the next time I stop the bus because she wanted to look at the ingredient. I immediately stopped and secured the bus. I got the water bottle from my lunch box and proceeded to bring it to her. Meanwhile she was looking through her purse for her glasses. While she was fidgeting through her purse she was talking to herself and saying something about how she'll never drink out of a bus drivers bottle unless she knows what's in the bottle.

I asked her if she wanted me to get her medical attention. Heck I didn't know if she was going to have an allergic reaction or possibly go into anaphylactic shock or what ever. I watched over her as she read the bottle. When she finished reading it she took off her glasses and put them back into her purse. I again asked her if she was alright. She said, "Yea I'm OK. I'm allergic to artificial flavoring and this is a natural extract."

I looked at her and said, "are you sure that your OK?" At which she replied, "Yes, now get this bus moving so that I can get home."

At that I replied," Yes mame." I resumed my route and got her home. Man was I glad that she didn't have any kind of reaction. I notified my dispatcher of what had happened and he requested that I write an incident report just to be safe. You never know what or how people are going to react in those situations. When I got back to the transit garage after my shift I wrote an incident report as per request by my dispatcher.

I hope that that passenger learned a lesson from that incident, I know that I did. Now any time one of my passengers speak about taking medicine or mention any thing about being thirsty, I automatically and immediately pick my bottle of water up and drink as sloppily as I can. I speak of how I back wash into the bottle and how awful the water tastes. If it's hot outside, I say the water is hot and tastes terrible. If the passenger seems like they aren't being deterred by that, I mention how I think I have a cold or the flu coming on just to keep them at bay. One time I even mentioned that I had numerous canker sores in my mouth, which I didn't, just to make sure that the passenger got my point. The moral of that story is "Please keep your hands out of the bus driver's lunch box and above all to leave their drinking bottles alone."

Chapter 18

CELL PHONES, DOCTORS AND THE BUS!!

There should be some form of law of what people, in this case we're talking about passengers, can talk about on their cell phones in public places. I really don't care to listen, but people think that they need to yell into their cell phones when they are riding on the bus. Some of the stuff that I hear is stuff that should be between them and their doctor. And in some cases their physiatrists'.

I've heard people talk on their cell phones about their jobs, religion, sports and any topic that you can name. One lady that was riding the bus was notifying relatives about the death of a relative, but she couldn't go into detail because she didn't want to go over her allocated monthly minutes on her phone.

One afternoon a lady, whom I refer to as "The Cell Phone Lady", was on the bus and her cell phone sounded. I remember this lady because she was rather obese and was dressed very professionally. When she boarded the bus she was very quite and reserved. On her cell phone she had one of those catchy ring-tones that sounded like a siren. There were about six other passengers on the bus and every one of them heard her cell phone ringing.

The lady was trying to answer the phone, but: obviously she didn't really know what button to push to answer it. As she's was fidgeting with the buttons, she is speaking rather loudly to herself about how she should have read the instructions more carefully. She finally got the phone to stop ringing and answered with a very loud "Hello." The other passengers went back to looking at the passing scenery or what ever they were doing before being interrupted by the obnoxious ring.

The lady, who had the cell phone, started her conversation with a very loud and robust laugh. She was speaking very loudly into her phone and really didn't seem to care who was listening to her conversation. It was an annoying situation right from the start. When her conversation started, one of the other passengers who was seated near her, got up from where he was sitting and moved toward the rear of the bus. Obviously he moved because of not wanting to be interrupted while he was enjoying his reading of the daily newspaper.

As I drove the bus and carried out normal operating procedures, the lady carried on with her conversation. The topic that she was conversing about was very graphic and detailed. She was relating to whom ever she was talking to about her recent visit to her doctor. I tried not to listen but she was seated only three feet away and I couldn't help it. At one of my stops, to let a lucky passenger off, I excused myself for interrupting her and asked her very politely if she could please keep her conversation down because she was talking rather loudly. She told the person whom she was speaking with to," hang on a sec." She then gave me a disgusting look and said to me in no uncertain terms to mind my own business. In a way I guess she was right.

As I drove she kept talking. My other passengers and I heard all about her boil on her left buttock that she just had lancet. She was talking about how painful it was and how fluids used to seep out of it. Zits baths and warm showers were some of the methods that she tried before consulting a physician. This was more than I need to know. She also went into great detail about how she couldn't wear lighter colored pants suits because the boil would break and ooze fluids. Speaking ever so loudly and clearly she was confining to her friend how the pain had gone away once she went to the doctor. The person to whom she was speaking to must have been asking questions about the procedure because the lady kept talking in greater detail about it.

This was one conversation I wished would end. Finally the cell phone lady reached up and pulled the chime line. Mine and the remaining passenger's wishes had come true. As I pulled up to the next closest bus stop the cell conversation came to an end and the cell phone lady stood up from her seated position. She was patiently waiting to disembark the bus. Before she got off the bus she turned toward me and the remaining passengers and said in a loud sarcastic voice, "Some people just don't respect others privacy."

I watched as the cell phone lady walked down the front stairs of the bus. I told her to watch her step and have a nice day. She had a light colored pant suit on and I couldn't help but notice as she walked away the telltale sign of her boil.

I said to myself, "Myself, drive the bus." As I started to drive away some of the other passengers were talking amongst themselves about what they had just witnessed and how rude that lady was acting. One of them even thanked me for requesting her to tone it down a bit. About that time one of the remaining passenger's cell phone rang. I and the other passengers stopped talking and watched to see what he was going to do. He answered the cell phone and said, "Hey man, I'm on the bus. I'll call you later." And then he disconnected and looked at us. I guess it was one of those moments when you just had to be there. We all started laughing. All I could think to myself was, at least someone learned something from what had happened.

The cell phone lady periodically rides my bus. Since that memorable day, thank God, she has never used her cell phone while she is riding on the bus. I know she still has one because I've seen her talking on it at the transfer points on numerous occasions. Before she boards the bus, she turns her cell phone off. What a novel idea.

Not wanting to put myself in a position that would make her or me uncomfortable; I put that bus ride and that loud cell phone conversation off limits. I know that it's going to make me look as if I'm nosey, but; There has been one question that I've been dying to ask her and that is, "Have you ever reread the instruction on how to use your cell phone?"

Chapter 19

FRUSTRATED WOMAN AND HER PSYCHIATRIST!!

A young woman in her mid twenties boarded my bus one day. I could tell by her body language that she was having a serious phone conversation with whom ever. As she boarded the bus, she flashed her monthly bus pass at me and sat down on the first seat of the bus. Why do people feel that they must sit in the first row of an empty bus is beyond me. Her cell phone was on speakerphone and I could hear the whole conversation. Not that I wanted to.

She was speaking to someone named Howard and it was obvious that Howard didn't want anything to do with her by the comments he was making. I heard Howard say, "Good bye and good riddance" and disconnect from the conversation. I could tell that the young woman was very distraught and frustrated from the way that the conversation had ended.

I looked at her and asked if she was alright. Her response was, "I love Howard."

Trying to be sensitive, I told her that maybe she should be telling that to Howard instead of me.

At that she said that she was not supposed to have any contact with Howard. I should have known better and my better judgment should have kicked in but I asked her "Why."

At that she said, "Howard is my Psychiatrist and has a restraining order against me."

I exclaimed, "He has a restraining order against you? For What?"

She sheepishly replied, "Stalking."

Not leaving well enough alone I said, "Let me get this straight. First of all, he's your Physiatrist. Then you said that he has a restraining order against you for stalking him. Did I hear you correctly?"

She replied, "Yes, but I love him!" Now I should have left well enough alone and just driven the bus, but: I had to ask, "Are you stalking him."

Her response was, "Yes." And might I add that she said it with no emotion or remorse.

I kept quiet the rest of the time that she was on the bus, but: I kept a close eye on her until she got off my bus. In a way, I was a little bit afraid of this woman. Heck, if I got too friendly, she might have taken it wrong and I might have became the affection of her life. And I sure didn't mean for that to happen. As I was driving, I said to myself, "Marty, just keep your mouth shut and just drive the bus. There are some things that you don't need to know or need to get involved in."

I see that young lady every now and then and wonder how her therapy is going. She really seems like a nice person, but; she does have some major issues. Every once in a while when she is on the bus alone I'm dying to ask her, "How's Howard doing?" But then the reality check comes back and tells me to shut up and just drive the bus.

Chapter 20

KIDS ARE SPOILED ROTTEN THESE DAYS!!

The kids now a day are spoiled rotten. They want everything and they want it now. It's not that they deserve it, it's that they expect it. Why should they pay their dues like everybody else because society owes it to them. I see young adults with substantial rolls of money. I'm talking about teenagers with a couple hundred dollars on them at all times. It's no wonder why kids are getting beat up und robbed. They flash those rolls around like nothing.

Cell phones have become a joke. Mommy and daddy give these toys for mommy and daddy convenience and their not doing the young adults any favors. I guess home is where most of the sociological problems start and that is where the blame can be placed, but it doesn't always work that way. It's always easier to blame someone else.

I was downtown at the transfer center one afternoon waiting for all the other buses to arrive so that we could depart. We always wait for all the buses to arrive just in case they have transfers for us. Then at specified times we all depart simultaneously. While I was waiting, there were three young male adults, maybe sixteen or seventeen years of age, sitting on bicycles and talking to one another.

I remember these kids by their bikes. These bikes looked to be expensive. I don't know a lot about bikes, but; I'm sure that these cost four or five hundred dollars each. I thought to myself, "Man I wished that I had one like that when I was a kid."

All the buses arrived and it was time to depart. As I started to pull out of the transfer center I observed two of the young men that were involved in the conversation riding off on their bikes. The Third young man was running after my bus and hailing me. I pulled over next to the curb and stopped the bus. The young man boarded the bus and put his bus fare in the fare-box. He then started to walk toward the rear of the bus toward some other students who were sitting back there. I noticed that his expensive bike that he was sitting on was lying on the ground at the transfer center next to a bench. The bike didn't have any chain, cable or lock securing it. My first thought was, "If he leaves that bike there like that, somebody going to steal it."

I said to the young man as he was walking toward the rear of the bus, "Young man if you leave that bike there like that someone is going to steal it." I was thinking that he is just a kid and doesn't think about stuff like that and maybe I could help.

He turned his head toward me and continued to walk toward the rear of the bus. As he walked he said, " I don't care; I stole it anyway."

I said, "You stole it?" The young man sat at the rear of the bus acting as if nothing had just happened. I watched in the mirror and he and his friends were having a carefree time talking about that bike. I was mad. I was mad at his arrogant attitude. I was mad because of his demeanor. And I was mad because he made me look like a fool.

I had driven for about three blocks and was thinking about what had just transpired. Then it dawned on me that we have cameras and video on the bus. I thought about where at the transfer center he and his pals were talking and where he had dropped the stolen bike. I was positive that my front door camera had picked up the whole event. Not only that but my inside camera and recorder had picked up his confession also. I didn't cause a scene with the kid that dropped the bike because that is not my job. I drive the bus. Instead I picked up my phone and notified my dispatcher. I informed them of what had happened and asked if they could pull the tapes and review it as possible evidence against this kid.

When I was talking on the phone to my dispatcher, I was speaking in a low voice. I didn't want to cause any trouble on the bus. The young man, who stole the bike, observed me speaking on the phone and started walking to the front of the bus. I could see by his kinesics that he was angry.

We were just three blocks away from the transfer center. I pulled the bus over and stopped by the curb. I put my four way flashers on and opened the front and rear doors of the bus. I did this just incase there was any trouble with this lad and incase any of the other passengers wanted to get off. I waited for the young man, who was now standing about two feet away from me, to speak. He said in an angry voice, "Did you call the cops on me?"

Well, I should have lied and said "No", but I didn't. I said, "No, I didn't call the police. What I did was call my dispatcher and he's going to call the police." We bus drivers really don't have anything to protect us. Heck I'm strapped in the seat and really can't move. My only protection would be my phone and my wits. I new that this kid was going to do something and he was going to do it to me. I should have kept my mouth shut, but; I was angry. When I was younger I used to Box and I know that I can take a punch, but; this was stupid of me because I don't get paid to fight. I get paid to drive the bus.

Sure enough I could see the kid taking a swing at me with his right hand. Seated in the seat, I instinctively put my right hand up to block and got in a boxers shell. That is a defensive position that protects you from punches that are thrown at you. The kids punch deflected off of my guarded arm and went by the way. I told the kid that if he takes another swing at me that I will defend myself. My left hand was cocked and ready. I didn't want to lose my job, but I'll darned if I going to sit there and get beat up by this kid.

Obviously the kid took me seriously and jumped off the bus. As he was running away from the bus he was turning his shirt inside out. He had one of those reversible shirts on that was white on one side and red on the other. I notified my dispatcher that the kid taken a swing and me and that I needed a police officer on the scene immediately.

A few minutes went by and my dispatcher came on the radio and asked if there was any imminent danger to myself or my passengers. I said, "No."

Dispatches response was, "The police are to busy to come out now. They will have a squad at the transit garage waiting for you when your shift is over. At that time you can fill the paperwork out." I asked if at least a police squad could go down to the transfer center and pick the kid up. Dispatches response was, "No all the Police squads are busy."

I then asked, "What about the mechanic down at the transfer center? Maybe he could go and get the bike and bring it in the transfer center garage." Dispatched response was, "The Transfer center's mechanic is off duty now, and there is nobody there."

By now I'm thinking "What a joke." Cars can park in bus stops, kids can steal bikes and passengers can take swings at bus drivers. Where are the police when you need them?

I finished my shift and returned to the transit garage. Sure enough, there was a police car with two officers in it waiting to take my statement. As I finished my paperwork one of the officers came up to my bus and said, "Sorry, we didn't respond when your dispatcher called, but; if there would have been imminent danger to you or your passengers no less than two squads would have responded. We were at the wake of a fellow officer and we were all paying our last respects to him together. Thank you very much for understanding." Man did I feel like a dummy now. I said, "No problem, now lets get this paper work done."

I informed dispatch that I was on the property and filling out the police reports. She acknowledged and told me to take my time. I informed the officers that I believed that the entire incident was picked up on my dash and interior camera. I though that they would be ecstatic about that news, but; they weren't. They seemed more interested in any info that I could give them. It was obvious to me that they wanted to speak with this kid. I also mentioned that the kid had told me that he had stolen the bike. They immediately asked if they could view the tapes. I contacted dispatch and a mechanic was sent out to my bus to retrieve the tape. The two police officers, my dispatcher and I went to the transit conference room to view the tapes.

We all sat waiting anxiously as the mechanic inserted the recorded tape into the recorder. There was a problem. It seems that there was an equipment malfunction and nothing had been recorded. I asked the mechanic if he could please check again. He did. Nothing was on the tape.

I finished the required paperwork with the officers. The said that they were a little bit disappointed, but; they were used to equipment problems like we had experienced. The told me that if I see the young man, that I was to notify my dispatcher and that they would contact the police. They requested that I not approach this individual by myself. I agreed. I thanked them for their time and again expressed sympathy for their fallen comrade.

Since that incident, I have never seen that young man or his other two friends again. I have seen the young adults who he was talking to on the bus, but; I have never mentioned anything to them about the incident. I figured that there was no need to get them involved by putting them in a position where they might get hurt. I myself learned an important lesson that day and that is, "Drive the bus and keep your comments to yourself."

Chapter 21

COLLEGE GIRLS!!

Our transit system services two local colleges. I always thought that the high school kids had issues, but; now that I'm dealing with college kids their pranks put all the high school pranks to shame. Most of the time the college kids are more interested in impressing members of the opposite sex than any thing else. Beer and sexual connotations are usually the root cause of most of their social problems.

As I pulled up to the bus stop I encountered two young ladies whom I know attend one of the colleges. I was on my first run of the day and it was very early in the morning. They both looked as if they were partying all night. I opened the front door and they both got on the bus. The first girl had an un-open bag of Cheeto snacks in her left hand as she put her dollar fare into the fare box with her right hand. I looked at her and glanced down at the bag of snacks. She looked back at me waiting for me to say something. I looked her in the face and said, "I don't want a mess on the bus. Please don't open those up." She turned and started to walk to the rear of the bus and said, "Ok. No problem. I understand." She than stopped at the standee line and waited for her friend.

The second girl had a lunch bag in her hands and was fumbling through it for her bus fare. I watched as she was looking in the bag, but; she was being careful not to let me see what the contents were in the bag. I waited as she kept digging and searching in the lunch bag with her hand for her bus fare. After waiting a minute or so, I said to her, "Is this going to take all day or what?" The second girl, who was standing by the standee line waiting, said to the girl fidgeting with the lunch bag, "Come on hurry up, lets go." The girl holding the lunch bag in her haste, accidentally ripped the bag open and its entire content spilled on the bus floor in front of me. The lunch bag's content included her bus fare in coin change and approximately seventy or eighty prophylactics. All the condoms were packaged in there factory packaging and none were open. As I looked down at the mound of multicolored and assorted varieties of condoms, I wondered, "What the heck was she doing with all these? Was this a supply for the dormitory or were these for her personal use." I started to read the wording on the packaging to myself. Some of the wording included ribbed, flavored, fantasy enhanced and erotic. About then a reality check kicked in and I said to myself, "Mind your own business and just drive the bus."

The girl who was holding the bag immediately bent over and hastily started picking up the fallen load. No pun intended. The girl who was standing by the standee line started laughing and turned to go sit down at the rear of the bus. There were no other passengers on the bus so I just sat there watching her pick up her pile of packaged condoms. I wanted to laugh but I didn't. The girl who was bent over and picking the mess up started laughing and looked and me and said, "I'm sorry, I'm hurrying." My comment to her was the same as I told her Cheeto toting companion. I said to her, "I don't want a mess on the bus. Please don't open those up." And her reply to me was, "Ok. No problem. I understand." Talk about Dejvu.

The girl who had gone to the rear of the bus appeared with a plastic bag and she gave it to the girl that was busy picking up the condom mess. The girl on the floor gladly took the bag and promptly started inserting all the condoms into the plastic bag.

With her hand she reached up to me and said, "Here's my bus fare." Well I usually don't except any money from the passengers, but; I made an exception this time and put the change in the fare-box for her. The girl that was on the floor got up and she and her friend, by now both of them were laughing hysterically, retreated to the rear seat of the bus. I couldn't hear their comments, but; I'm sure that they were justifying their embarrassing moment.

The remainder of the bus ride went smooth and I got the girls to their destination, the college. They exited through the rear door and said,"Thank you." My reply was, Have a nice day"

Every once in a while I see those two girls and I wonder what their thinking when they see me. One time they got on the bus and one of them had a rather large suitcase. As they got on the bus I joked with them and said, "Girls, please don't empty the suitcase on the bus floor." We all laughed and one of they said, "Ok. No problem. We understand." It's funny how thing go around in full circle.

Chapter 22

Young couple fighting on bus!!

A young couple was on the bus one day and they were arguing about something. I interrupted them numerous times and told them both that I don't allow swearing on my bus. They didn't care and kept it up. I watched in the mirror as the argument escalated. I could tell that it wasn't going to take long before the verbal argument to turn physical. I got on the loudspeaker and asked them to please stop because they were annoying the other passengers. The couple stopped arguing at my plea.

The female got up and moved to the seat across the aisle from the male. I could see in the mirror that the male was very tall and skinny and the female was short. They both sat in their seats not saying a word. After a short ride the male pulled the chime line. I stopped at the next stop and the male got up from his seat and started to go to the back door of the bus. The female got up from her seat and immediately went to the front door of the bus. This irritated the male. He turned toward the front of the bus and walked purposely toward the front door by the female.

They both exited the bus exchanging words. As they were walking away from the bus the male grabbed the female by her shoulder, spun her around and proceeded to punch her smack in the face with a closed fist. They were no more than five feet way from the bus and I not only saw the punch, but; it was hard enough that I heard it. The male then started walking away leaving the girl standing there alone. She was crying and her nose was bleeding.

I told the girl to get on the bus and she did. All the other passengers, there were about ten, that were on the bus were now talking about what had just happened. The girl sat down on the front seat of the bus and I drove off. I glanced in my side rearview mirrors and could see the young man was still walking away and not looking back. He didn't care. I thought to myself, what a tough guy he thinks he is.

One passenger offered her his cell phone so that she could call the police. She declined his offer. I contacted my dispatcher and described the events that had just happened. I was told to write an incident report when I returned to the garage. I offered the young lady, who was now bleeding profusely from her nose, a roll of paper towel and my garbage can.

As I drove my bus route I spoke with the young lady. I told her that she didn't have to put up with that. I mentioned to her that she is a good looking young lady and should find someone who would appreciates her for what she is. I said, "You need to find someone that will treat you like a lady and not like a punching bag. Are you two married?" She shook her head no and replied sheepishly, "But I love him."

I said, "You realize that love goes both ways. No one has the right to hit anybody. Love shouldn't hurt." She replied, "I know, but; sometime he gets mad."

I drove along and dropped passengers off at their stops. When I got to the end of the line it was only the young lady and me left on board. The young lady and I chatted for a bit. We spoke about the weather and the up coming holiday. She mentioned that she had enrolled in classes at a local college to insure that she would have a better future in front of her. She impressed me with her positive attitude. I thought to myself, "Well, maybe she actually is on the right track." I avoided mentioning anything about her misfortune and her need to find another boyfriend. I figured that I had said too much already. I didn't want to preach to her, I think she got the point. I continued with the route and ended up in the area where her altercation had taken place. She pulled the chime line and I pulled the bus over to let her disembark. As she was getting off the bus, I told her to think about what I had said. She said, "Thanks for caring and she would give some serious thought to our conversation."

As I started to pull away from the curb, the young woman started to run. I watched as she ran to the waiting arms of her boyfriend who was standing about thirty yards away from the bus stop. This was the same fellow, who not more than a half hour ago, punched her in the face. He must have been hiding behind one of the many trees in the area because I never saw him. If I would have, I would have told her. I pulled the bus over to the curb and watched as they embraced. I'm thinking to myself, "Man does she have a lot to learn." As I again pulled the bus away from the curb and merged into traffic I glanced back and watched as the two lovebirds strolled away holding each others hand. I shook my head in disbelief and mutter to myself, "Whatever."

After completing my route for the day, I returned to the transit garage and wrote an incident report describing in detail my account of the occurrence. The next day I was assigned the same route and who should I encounter, but; the same couple. As they boarded the bus I noticed that she had an unusual amount of love hickeys on her neck that weren't there yesterday. I said to myself, "Mind your own business and drive the bus." When she boarded the bus she nodded her head to acknowledge me and then went to sit at the rear of the bus. Her boyfriend boarded the bus, paid both of their fares and bid me "good morning". I politely acknowledged him. I didn't say what I really wanted to. He walked to the rear of the bus and sat down next to the young lady. They both acted as if nothing had happened. I watched in the mirror as they sat there. He put his arm around her and she looked as content as could be. They rode the bus to the far end of the route and disembarked. I watched as they walked away.

About one month later I was reading the local newspaper and read an article about a domestic violence case. It seems that a young man was beating up his live in girl friend and things got out of control. The story told of how a young woman fought back by picking up a steak knife and plunging the knife into her lover's chest. The article went on about how the young woman might be charged with a felony because the young man was not expected to survive the injuries. Above the article that I was reading was a picture of the young lady that I spoken with that day on the bus. All I could think of was, "What a waste."

I have never read anything else in the local newspaper about that incident, nor have I seen either one of the two again. I do not know what the out come was, but: I can say to myself that I sincerely tried to help.

Chapter 23

To busy listening to his radio!!

We bus drivers usually know if someone is on the wrong bus. Believe it or not, contrary to public beliefs, some of us do remember things. A few clues that are dead give aways are: how the kids are dressed; what time of day it is; what day it is or perhaps if the kid has special need. I'm not stereo -typing, but; certain schools allow kids to wear different styles. For instance if a kid is wearing a military uniform he goes to the High school on the west side of town. If the kid is wearing Gothic it's a real good bet that they go to the high school on the south side of town. If the young adult is pushing a baby carriage she probably goes to a the alternate high school downtown. It's a little system that I use. Most of the time I use my memory, it hardly ever fails me. I have a real good memory of faces and places.

I'm downtown one morning and I am driving a route that is a split shift route. I work that shift from six o'clock in the morning until eight thirty in the morning. I than get a five hour break and I do not have to be back to the transit garage until one thirty in the afternoon. That shift ends at seven forty three. If I'm lucky enough to have that route the entire week I automatically get the weekend off.

Its setup that way because of the shift being so long. It's not really that bad of shift to work once you get used to it.

A kid gets on my bus and I notice that he is getting on the wrong bus. By the way that is dressed I'm sure that he goes to the school on the north side of town and I'm going to be headed south. When the buses on this shift meet downtown there are a total of twelve buses assembled. Six of the buses head in a northerly pattern and the remaining six head in a southerly pattern or a variation to encompass the entire city.

As the student was putting his fare into the fare-box I looked him in the face and asked him if he was on the right bus. He looked at me with a blank stare on his face and said nothing. My impression was that he acted like I was annoying him. He than walked a couple rows back and sat down. I noticed that he had a baseball cap on and that under the cap he had earphones on. He was listening to music or whatever. I was sitting in the driver's seat and turned to him. I got his attention and I motioned with my hands toward my ears hoping that he would take his earphones off or at least lower the volume so he could hear me.. I said, "Young man the buses are going to be leaving shortly. Let me know what your destination is because there is a probability that you are on the wrong bus. If you are on the wrong bus, I'll direct you to the right one so that you get to your destination in the shortest time possible. Otherwise if your on the wrong bus, your going to take a ride to the end of the line and have to wait about forty minutes or so for another bus to arrive." His way of acknowledging me was; he reached toward the I-pod that was attached to his belt and turned the volume up. I said, "OK, have a nice ride."

I got to the end of the line, and lo and behold, I had only one passenger left on the bus, the kid with the earphone on. I stopped the bus and started to do my paperwork.

The young man came to the front of the bus and said to me, "I seem to be on the wrong bus, how long before we leave to go back downtown? My response was, "I don't go back downtown."

He said, "Why didn't you tell me that before we left, so that I could get on the other route that headed north?"

I sarcastically said to him, "I tried talking to you twice, but; you seemed to think that your music was more important than what I had to say. I'm sorry; I'm not going back downtown, I'm headed back to the garage because I'm off duty now. What I'll do is drop you off at the closest transfer point and you'll have to wait for a bus that's headed toward downtown or transfer to one that's headed north." I would have given him a ride if he hadn't treated me like a fool. He immediately took his cell phone out of his pocket and called someone.

I notified dispatch and told them that I had a student on the bus that was trying to go north. Dispatched suggested that it would be OK to give him a ride to his destination. My reply was, "No, I'll explain why, when I return to the garage." The Dispatcher's reply was," 10-4." I dropped the student off at a safe and secure transfer point and suggested that he use his cell phone to call whoever, so they know where he's at and he was going to be late. He stormed off the bus and sat down on a bench. He knew that he had a long wait and took out a novel and started to read it.

I returned to the garage and explained to my dispatcher what had happened and they said that they were going to pull the tape and review it. They also suggested that I write an incident report, detailing my account of the incident. I did. My route supervisor reviewed the tape and said that I did nothing wrong. Heck, all that kid would have had to do was answer me. Now, I'm filling out paperwork and he is sitting on a park bench waiting for a bus. I hope he learned a lesson. I know I did. Next time an incident like that happen, I'm not moving the bus until I get an answer.

Chapter 24

Could you drop me off at the Bank?

One thing I've figured out about driving a bus and dealing with the public is: "Don't try to understand things that you don't need to understand. Just drive the bus." Sound like gibberish, but; there's a lot to be said about it, for instance.

Last October, I vividly remember an elderly gentleman who got on the bus. It was autumn and the leaves were brilliantly colored. The air was crisp and the midday sun was shinning. As I drove my assigned route, I was enjoying the multi-colored spectacle that Mother Nature was putting on. I had no incidents during my shift up to the point when the elderly man had gotten on the bus. Everything seemed to be going smoothly. When I say smoothly, I mean nothing out of the ordinary. The elderly gentleman bid me good morning, showed me his monthly bus pass and sat down in the front seat of the empty bus. His demeanor suggested to me that he was on a mission.

I remember having this fellow on my bus in the past. The only thing different today was that he was alone. He usually is accompanied by his wife. I know that the lady is his wife because she always mentions that he is the love of her life and that they have been married for over fifty years. The elderly man is usually quiet and keeps to himself while riding the bus. His wife on the other hand is just the opposite. When she is on the bus, she is usually very vocal and outgoing. She is friendly with the other passengers and knows most of those who ride the bus by their first name. She has a quality where once she speaks to you, you remember her and think of her as a friend. She treats everyone the same and from what I can tell doesn't prejudge people. Many of the young adults like her because of her outspokenness.

On the other hand, the way she treats her husband is a lot different than the way she treats her bus riding social acquaintances. He is obviously the love of her life, but; at times she treats him like he is a child. When she is with him on the bus she tells him what seat to sit in, where they are going and when their getting off. He never argues or disagrees with her and always lets her have her way. I think that was because he is very well trained by her. She told me one time that they have been married almost fifty years and they plan on celebrating another fifty. I remember the look of satisfaction and approval on his face when she said that and I thought to myself how wonderful that was. Even though he was pleased by her comment, he had a look in his eyes that bewildered me. Was the look in his eyes the look of love, or was it the look of "Somebody please help me!" I'm not sure.

Well anyways I drove off and continued with my scheduled route. The elderly gentleman started up a conversation with me. A bus driver is supposed to limit his conversations with the passengers to route information only. That is very difficult for me to do. Being the social butterfly that I am, I responded to his comments with a series of "Yes's", "No ways" or an "Occasional grunt."

After about two or three minutes of him doing all the talking and me doing the listening, the conversation got really interesting. He was telling me that his wife didn't want him leaving the house and going out on his own because she thinks that he was forgetting too many things. He said, "She doesn't want me to leave the house and end up getting lost. I told her that I was fully capable of taking care of myself and that she worried too much. I'm going out today and do some errands and prove to myself and her that I still can be trusted. She and I usually don't argue; but, this time I'm going to prove her wrong!"

I was starting to get worried now. I'm thinking why is he telling me this? Is there something that I should know? Being the inquisitive guy that I am, I asked him where he was headed to. That question that I asked, actually lead the conversation between the two of us to talk about route information. The conversation went something like this:

The old gentleman," I'm going to the bank. Hey, could you drop me off at the bank?"

I said to him," Sure, what bank are you going to?"

With a puzzled look on his face the old gentleman replied," Mmmm, I forget the name of the bank and what street it's on, but; I remember that it's on the corner with the stop lights."

I said," Sir, there are a lot of banks in town that are on a corner with stop lights. What else can you tell me?"

He immediately replied, "I know that there's a tavern kiddie corner from the bank."

Quizzing him I asked, "Do you happen to know the name of the tavern?"

His reply didn't amaze or astound me when he said, "No."

Now I'm starting to get worried. I'm start thinking about what he was telling me about his wife's apprehension and concerns with him getting lost. I glanced into my mirror and saw that the elderly gentleman was just sitting there looking out the window. He was supposed to be thinking about where the bank was, but: he seemed more content on enjoying the bus ride. This was not the same fellow who not more than five minutes ago was talking my ear off and telling me things that he thought I should know. It seemed a shame to bother him, but; I needed to find out where he was going. I said to him, "Excuse me sir. OK, so you're going to the bank. What I understand is that you don't know the bank's name or where it's at. Is that correct?"

I was looking at him through the reflection in my interior mirror as I drove the bus. His glanced at my reflection and said, "Yea, I guess so."

You also said that the bank was on a corner with the stop lights and kiddie corner from the bank is a tavern. Is there anything else that you can remember about that location?"

He looked at me and said," There is a old gas station on the other corner where I used to bring my car to get gas and the house that we live in is next door to the gas station."

I thought to myself for a moment, trying to grasp everything that the elderly gentleman had told me and I came to what I thought to be a logical conclusion. I said to him, "So what your telling me is that you live across the street from the bank. Is that right?"

"Yea", he anxiously replied. He was looking at me as if I were a person who had finally deciphered an ancient secret code or more important to him where he was going.

Looking at him in the reflection in the interior mirror I said to him, "Where do you live?"

I really should have been prepared for the answer that he was about to give, but I figured and expected to hear anything.

He said, "By the bus stop where you picked me up in front of my house."

I looked at him and he was staring back at me. The look on his face was one of not having a care in the world. I didn't want to hurt his feelings, but: rather I wanted to try to figure out where he was going or more important if he knew where he was going.

Talking to myself, but out loud, I said to him "So, I picked you up at the bus stop in front of the bank that you wanted to go, right?" His facial expression changed when I said that. It dawned on him that he didn't have to get on the bus and could have walked to the bank that was across the street from where he lived. A look of disgust came over the elderly mans face. He said nothing and turned and stared out the bus window looking at the autumn surroundings. The conversation ended and I drove the bus on my established route and got to the end of the line. I was right on schedule and had a few minutes before I needed to retrace my route and head back downtown.

The elderly gentleman was sitting on the bus just looking out of the bus window. I could tell that he was thinking about something. I didn't want to interfere with him so since I had a few minutes, I got off the bus and went and sat on a bus stop bench that I was parked by. The autumn colors were brilliant and I was enjoying the view. As I sat there, I couldn't help but to think about the elderly gentleman sitting on my bus. I thought to myself; everybody makes silly mistakes and are no worst for the wear, but: he seemed to be taking it rather hard.

The time at the end of the line flew by and I had to resume my route. I got on the bus and sat down in the driver's seat. As I was putting my seatbelt on: I turned to the elderly gentleman and asked him if he was OK. He said, "Yea, I'm OK."

As I turned the bus around and started back on my trip downtown the elderly man started to speak as we drove on. I thought to myself that this was the fellow who had gotten on my bus and was so talkative and friendly. He was happy go lucky and talking to me about nothing in particular. The topics that he spoke about varied from the weather, to sports and life in general. As I drove on, I listened to his wisdom and his tales.

As we approached the bus stop corner where I had picked him up earlier, I sensed a changed in his vocal tone. He said to me in a very serious voice, "You know, its hard to grow old. When we make mistakes when were young, we learn lessons from those mistakes. The same is true when you get older. I learned something about myself today. I'm not going to tell you what I learned because I think that you already figured it out. I'm lucky to have a good woman like my wife and I think that I need to listen to her more no matter what I think. Do me a favor, don't mention any of this to her because I don't want her to worry." I said to him, "Mention anything about what?" He gave me a wink of his eye and a nod of approval and went back to looking out of the bus window.

A half of block before his bus stop he pulled the chime line signaling that he needed to get off of the bus. I drove up to the bus stop across the street from where I picked him up and stopped the bus. I then kneeled the bus and opened the door. The elderly gentleman got up from his seat and walked to the front of the bus. He stopped and extended his hand in friendship. I shook his hand which was a rare gesture for me because I try to avoid physical contact with my passengers. I do this because I do not know their hygiene habits. After shaking my hand he disembarked the bus. I told him to take his time and be careful getting off the bus.

As he was getting off the bus, I was checking out the corner that he had described to me. Sure enough there was a bank on the corner with stop lights. Kiddie corner from the bank was a tavern and across the street from the bank was an abandoned gas station. The gas station obviously has been out of business for many years, but it was still there. Nestled next to the closed gas station was a well kept older house. I said to myself, "O.K that's where he lives."

Every time after that day, whenever I saw the elderly gentleman he was accompanied by his wife. Nothing changed. She always told him where to sit and he obliged her. As I would drive the bus and it's passengers on the established route, the man's wife would talk and carry on her business and he would sit there and look out the moving buses window as if he hadn't a care in the world. I never had another conversation with the elderly man again; but every time that he would get on or off my bus, the elderly gentleman would give me a wink with his eye. I sure that that was his was of saying that everything was OK.

Chapter 25

ANIMALS ON THE BUS!!

It's a fact that people love their pets. Our family has a pet dog that we treat like a family member. He is named "Buddy" and is a hundred pound plus Rotreiller, fully house broken and gentle as a lamb. Even though we enjoy his company at home, we don't feel obligated to him to take him everywhere we go. People think that they need to take their pets on the bus with them. It's a known fact that when a pet has a bodily function to release, they don't care who's around, they do what comes naturally and what happens, happens.

I've encountered a variety of God's creatures, were talking animals, on the bus. I think some of my passengers could fall into this category, but; I won't go there. This gathering includes; dogs, cats, snakes, mice, rats, ferrets, guinea pigs, fish, insects and numerous members of the bird family. The most common bird that is carried on the bus is chicken. Yes, people have brought live chickens on the bus, but; most of the time when chicken is brought on the bus it comes in a boxed container with a picture of the Colonel Sanders on it.

One day a guy got on the bus carrying a burlap bag. I said, "Hey what's in the bag?" As he finished putting his fare in the fare box he turned to me and said," A seventy pound; six foot python."

I said," What?" He told me that I had nothing to worry about and that he brings his pet snake on the bus with him all the time. I said," This is the first time that you've been on my bus with a burlap bag." At which he said, "I know, I usually carry the snake around my neck hidden under my jacket." I contacted my dispatcher and told them what I was just told. They told me that I should tell him that he can bring his pet snake on the bus only if it's in a secure bag or case. The snake guy agreed and said that it won't happen again.

Its kind of funny how I notice this fellow more often now when he gets on my bus. My first inclination is to look to see if he's wearing a jacket and my second is to ask if he has his pet snake with him. He reassures me periodically that he will never bring his snake on the bus unless he has it in a burlap bag. I'm a trusting sole ,but; I still check every time he gets on my bus. Funny thing is that he knows that I'm looking to catch him with that snake.

Many of the creatures that end up on the bus are on their way to the Veterinarians or the pet groomer's office. Most of the time, these critters are placed in secure cages. When I say secure, I mean any container that their owner's feels will keep them contained. In other words not running or flying around the interior of the bus. The most common containers used includes; Approved pet carriers; Covered baskets; cardboard boxes; and burlap gunny sacks. Of course, all these are suitable unless were talking fish. Then water must be present and that alone and a moving bus can be disastrous.

We live on the shores of Lake Michigan and at certain times of the year, fishing is a very popular past time of many area residents. I get quite a few kids on the bus with fishing poles, nets and tackle boxes. I figure if a kids going fishing, let them. After all there are a lot of other activities that they could be doing that they shouldn't be doing and fishing will help keep them out of trouble.

At certain times of the year it's easy and not uncommon to catch some very large fish right from the areas piers and break waters. The boat harbor that we have is rather large and used to port ocean going vessels. The harbor itself is approximately sixty feet deep in areas. We have numerous marinas' that cater to offshore fisherman and these marinas have a viable fleet of charter boats that make a good income from fishing. I've had to turn down many fisherman from getting on the bus because they wanted to bring their catch aboard the bus. Like I said if it's in a secure contain they can bring it on the bus, if not: the answer is no. I remember a couple kids who were waiting at the bus stop holding three of four rather large King Salmon that that had caught. The problem was that they were carrying the fish in a fishing net. I told them that I could not let them on the bus carrying the fish like that because they would make a wet smelly mess on the bus. I then told the kids that if they waked home that they could show their catch off.

As I drove away, I glanced in the mirror and saw the kids walking away. They were carrying the fish in a way that passing motorist's couldn't help but to see them. They seemed happy with the out come; but, not as happy as I was.

Quite a few resourceful bus riders try to smuggle their precious pets on the bus past the bus driver. These passengers usually think that their clever, I use that term loosely, and the bus driver is an ignoramus. These clandistic passengers think that all they have to do is to hide their pets underneath their shirts or jackets. Regardless of what many passengers think, the bus driver wants to be and is usually aware of what is on the bus. Were concerned, not only for our safety, but; the safety of all the other passengers as well.

I remember a young lady, maybe in her mid-twenties, who rode the bus regularly. One day she got on the bus at the downtown transfer center and told me that she was bringing her pet dog to the Veterinarians office because the dog was acting funny. She then opened her coat and showed me a puppy. I'm not a Veterinarian but I could tell by looking at that puppy that it was sick. I said to her, "Are you sure that you want to carry that puppy in your shirt like that?"

She immediately replied, "Oh, He'll be fine, I always carry him like that. I promise that I'll keep him in my shirt and will not take him out to bother the other passengers."

I again said, "That dog doesn't look too well. Do you think it's a good idea to have him in your shirt?" She again insisted that everything was going to be fine and I was not to worry because she had things under control.

I looked her in the face and said, "I like puppies, but; All I'm saying is I don't want that dog making a mess on my bus".

"I know", she replied.

Instead of me insisting that she put the puppy in a box or whatever, I took her word that everything was going to be fine. I said to myself, "Have a little faith in her. She knows her puppy not you." It's against transit rules to have a dog on the bus unless it's a seeing eye dog. Its not that I try to break or bend the rules, it's that I try to accommodate my passengers. I try to use good judgment and sometimes what I think is good turns out to be bad.

As I started to pull the bus out of the downtown transfer center someone pulled the chime line. I immediately looked into my interior rearview mirror and saw the young lady who had the puppy hidden in her shirt walking frantically toward the front of the bus. I noticed that she had a disgusting look on her face. Still gazing into the mirror, I glanced at the front of her shirt. Yep, you guessed it, the puppy had gotten sick while she was holding it within her shirt. About the time that the young lady made it to the front of the bus, a horrible stench was filling up the bus.

As I stopped the bus, the young lady looked at me and said, "I'm so sorry, I so sorry!" I didn't have time to answer her because my eyes started to water from the smell of puppy urine and puppy fecal matter. No matter how cute that puppy was, the smell of its body fluids were horrible. I felt really bad for that young woman too. She had a shirt full of an ungodly mess.

Wanting to get the smell out of the bus, I opened all the doors and windows. I didn't want to have to call my dispatcher and tell them of what had happened. The other buses had departed and I was the only bus in the transfer center. The young lady had run, with the puppy still in her shirt, to the far end of the transfer center where there was a grassy island. I watched as she took the now wet puppy and put it on the grass.

I don't know how women do it but the young lady took her shirt and bra off in one motion without exposing herself to the world. She was now wearing a sweatshirt that she had obviously been carrying in her hand bag. I know that she took those items off because she was holding them in each hand and frantically shaking them out. As I closed the bus doors and started to drive away I said to myself, "Yeah, everything is going to be fine, trust me."

It took about an hour for the bus to air out and to lose the puppy scents. Everything was fine and nobody was any worst for the wear except for an occasion comment from some of the newly boarded passengers. I drove the bus and didn't even respond. Heck I didn't even want to make a smart comment about it. I did that day learn a valuable lesson, but: I'm sure that young lady learned on too.

Chapter 26

Hey, discipline the kid will ya?

People discipline their children in different ways. My mom always told me that my butt is there because moms and dads needed a place to spank their kids, so a long time ago God thought about it and gave everyone a conveniently padded place. Needless to say when I was a kid, I still consider myself one only bigger, I got my share of well deserved spankings. My mom never used her closed fists to discipline her children although I think at times she wanted to. She had really good hand and eye coordination hitting her intended target, our butts, with her hand. Now that I drive a bus and I have the opportunity to see a variety of ways of how parents discipline their children. Let me first say that anytime that a child is reprimanded by an adult and that adult uses a closed fist and a series of punches; that adult needs to reconsider the consequence of their actions. They defiantly need some form of counseling.

Let me be a little bit sarcastic, not that I ever am, and say that I love it when parents discipline their children on the bus. Yea, I really enjoy having a crying and screaming kid on the bus. Some people believe that the time to punish a misbehaving child is immediately after the infraction, I like that the best, while; other parents let the misbehaving acts build up to the point that everyone one in the vicinity of the misbehaving child wants to discipline the child themselves. Either way the child gets what they have coming to them. I understand the fact that it's their children and that they can correct the child how they see fit. There is a multitude of books published on how a kid should be disciplined and it's amazing on how many people buy these books and use the books methods. However, I wish that people wouldn't try to practice any of these methods on the bus out in public.

One day I'm sitting at the end of the bus line waiting to resume my route. I had a few minutes before I had to leave so I figured that I'd take a quick look at the daily sports page. Obviously for safety reasons we can't read and drive the bus at the same time, so any chance that we bus drivers get to read, work on a puzzle, eat or whatever: we do. We bus drivers aren't allowed to have personal radios playing either because they could be a distraction to our driving. I had just started reading an article in the sports section when I noticed that some people walking my way. I really didn't give it much mind because it was a pleasant day outside and a good day to be out for a walk enjoying the outdoors. The group of people that I observed appeared to be a mom, dad and child. As they were approaching me I noticed that the Mom was pushing a stroller with a toddler aboard and Dad was holding the hand of the child. The child appeared to be approximately seven or eight years of age. Everything appeared to be normal and nothing out of the ordinary so I went back to my article.

As the group neared me I looked up from my paper and I noticed that the child, whose hand was being held by the man, was misbehaving. The man actually was holding the child by the wrist and not by the hand as I originally thought. The lady or Mom was causally pushing a stroller with the smiling toddler aboard who was occasionally sucking on a bottle, meanwhile; the dad on the other hand was dealing the misbehaving child. As the group passed by me I witness something I just couldn't believe.

The man was holding the child by the wrist to control the child because the child was acting like a brat. The child would fall to his knees and the man would stop and gently pick the child up and try to continue walking. The child did not want to standup and walk. What the child would do was scream and swear at the man while letting his little body go limp causing his body to fall to the ground. His actions would make the man stumble and nearly fall over the child. I must say, that man had more patients than I do. The man was being very tolerant and self composed as the child continued his little temper tantrums.

I was thinking to myself, "Man, if I ever did anything like that when I was a kid I'd have the sorest butt in town. That kid needs a good spanking."

The kid throughout his little tantrum was looking at me. It was as if he was saying, "Look what I can do. Ha, Ha, Ha." His body language and his eyes were telling a story without him saying a word. Mom followed closely behind the man and the boy as she pushed the toddler in the stroller. The patient dad acted as if nothing out of the ordinary was happening.

I watched as the man and child walked past me. The kid knowing that he had an audience continued with his uncontrolled behavior. At one point the child stuck his tongue out at me. Hey, I didn't do nothing to that kid to deserve that. Maybe he noticed me staring at him because I was just mesmerized by his actions. I guess that the child wanted to show me who was the boss. Whatever.

The child stopped in dad's stride and paused as if he was going to drop to the ground again. The dad stopped walking and stood there holding the child's wrist. The child just stood there as if he was thinking of what misbehaved action he could do next. A few seconds went by and as mom walked by pushing the toddler in the stroller; without warning the mischievous child broke free from dad's grip and lunged at the toddler in the stroller. He ran into the stroller so hard that the stroller tipped over.

While that was going on dad tried to control the child, while; mom was up righting the stroller. The toddler in the stroller started crying because he was startled and had dropped his bottle. Mom, after up righting the stroller, was anxiously checking out the toddler to make sure that he didn't get hurt by his siblings actions. By now dad had gained control of the child again by grabbing his wrist. Dad was asking the mom if the baby was O.K. as he pulled the misbehaving child away from the stroller. At that point the misbehaving child started laughing uncontrollably as if he did something that was funny. Dad was standing there upright holding the child's left wrist with his right hand and was looking at mom taking care of the toddler. The look on dad face finally gave an expression of anger.

Again, I'm just sitting there watching the whole show. I couldn't believe my eyes what happened next. While dad was busy watching mom, the mischievous child took his free right hand and with a hook like punching motion hit dad directly in the groin area. Needless to say, Dad was surprise by the sucker punch and doubled over in obvious agonizing pain. Mom witnessed the punch and immediately left the stroller and went to her husband' side to comfort him and supposedly give some kind of aid. It took a few seconds for Dad to regain his composure. He gaspingly told her that he was alright and she put her arm around him to comfort him.

About now I'm thinking that dad, after that sucker punch, was going to give that child a well deserved spanking and I didn't want to miss it. But no, that was not going to happen. What this father figure did next was after composing himself. He stood there a few seconds staring down at the naughty child. While this was going on, I glanced at my watch and realized that I had to get going on my bus route. After thinking and regaining his self composure, the dad bent down while still holding the child's left wrist with his right hand. When he bent down he was looking the misbehaving child face to face and eye to eye. What I'm hoping is that this guy doesn't start beating the kid. It's clear to me that this child is in dire need of counseling or something.

What the dad did next surprised me. The dad in a very calm voice said to the naughty child, "Young man, when we get home, you're getting a time out for your actions."

I said to myself, "A time out? What; is this guy nuts or what? This kid defiantly needs a good spanking." Again as I said earlier, all people discipline their children as see fit. My opinion is that this man and women are doing a disservice to that young child. A time out, I can't believe it.

I headed back to my bus and resume my route. When I drive the bus I try to concentrate on my driving and not be distracted by daydreams. I couldn't get the thought out of my head about that series of incidents that happened and how that man and women handled them. I started second guessing myself. Hey, my wife and I raised four children and they all turned out alright. Maybe my wife and I should have tried the time out method. Nah, I got spankings when I was naughty and I sure wasn't going to deprive my children of spankings. I sure that if you ask my kids what method they would have preferred for punishment when they were naughty as kids, I guessing that they all would have emphatically have preferred the time out method over the spanking method that we applied. Tough, they can do what they want when they have their own kids to discipline. My wife and I did it our way so get over it.

Chapter 27

BOOGERS! BREAKFAST OF CHAMPIONS!!

Many of my bus passengers have a problem with controlling or dealing with their bodily functions. Now bodily functions can mean a lot of different things. We all have orifices on our bodies where secretions of bodily fluids or gasses escape. These bodily functions are a part of our everyday life. A lot of times many of my bus passengers haven't a clue to the fact that their doing anything wrong with secretions. Yea, I know that bodily functions are a part of everyone needs, but; some of the mannerisms need to be done in the privacy of their own homes if one wants to pursue them. I've experienced numerous individuals doing acts that make me want to vomit. Again, I understand that there are numerous and vast reason why people ride the bus, but: there is a time and a place for everything.

A man got on my bus one day and sat down in the front seat directly across from my driver's seat. It's that front seat thing again. The guy was perhaps in his mid-thirties and by the way he was dressed, I could tell that perhaps hard times had fallen on him. His clothes were dirty and wrinkled and his hair looked like it was combed with his fingers rather than with a comb. When he put his bus fare into the fare box, I noticed that his fingers were nicotine stained. When he past by me to sit down in his chosen seat, I caught a distinct odor of booze and cigarettes. I didn't want to strike up a conversation with him; all I wanted to do was give him a bus ride to his destination.

As I drove the bus I kept a close eye on this fellow. I did this because we bus drivers need to be aware of our surrounding for our safety. I scan my interior mirrors and view the bus coach instinctively regardless if I know that there are any passengers sitting at the back of the bus or not. In addition to keeping tract of the inside the bus, more importantly, I need to know what's going on out side around the bus. Driving a bus keeps you on your toes.

At one point I looked to my right and glanced at my lone passenger. I watched as the man sat there picking boogers out of his nose and placing them in his mouth. After placing the boggers in his mouth, he was chewing on them as if they were gum or candy. I almost gagged. Consumption of bodily fluids, in this case boogers, is unacceptable in public or private. In fact I don't think that it's a good diet no matter how you look at it. I had to say something to him because I knew if I didn't he would do it again. I said to the man, "sir would you please use your handkerchief!" His head turned and looked at me. I startled him with my comment and I think that I caught him off guard. What the man did next was to lean forward and reached behind his back with his right hand. Just as quickly as his hand went back behind him, his hand came back in front, clutching a handkerchief. His actions reminded me of how a magician produces a hanky when they are performing magic tricks. He did that pretty fast.

The man did not say a word, but rather; just sat there clutching the hanky as he stared out of the bus window. Perhaps a little embarrassed because of what I saw him doing. I figured that I had gotten my point across and that the man would use his handkerchief rather eat his boggers. Wrong!

As I drove the bus I occasionally glanced at the man. Yes the man was using the handkerchief to blow his nose into, but; he was now using his handkerchief as if it were a lunchbox. Let me explain. After he blew his nose into the hanky, he would use his thumb and forefinger of his right hand to pick up a bogger and eat it. Now I'm really getting sick. I'm trying to drive the bus and at the same time ignore my bogger eating passenger. I had to say something again, but what? While I'm thinking of what to say the chime goes off signaling for me to stop at the next stop. Since I had only one passenger it was easy for me to figure out who it was. The man was going to get off my bus. So I said to myself, "don't say nothing just ignore him he'll be off the bus and gone in a minute or so."

As I drove up to the next bus stop and pulled up to the curb to let my bogger eating passenger off, the man said, "I sorry sir, I need the next bus stop please. I pulled the cord too early."

Being a professional, I turned and looked at him and said, "OK, no problem thing like that happens all the time." I pulled the bus away from the curb and headed for the next bus stop. I still didn't say anything because all I cared about was that he was getting off my bus. Bus stops are usually every two blocks. Bus stop placement is dictated by traffic flow and availability of parking. In layman's terms, bus stops are placed where a bus can safely stop and either pickup or drop off passengers. Just my luck, I was on a stretch where the next bus stop was three blocks down because of traffic patterns.

"Just look ahead and drive," I kept saying to myself. As I drove on toward the next bus stop, I came upon an intersection controlled by traffic lights. The traffic light turned yellow as I was approaching and rather than drive through it, as I wanted to do, I stopped. No sense in getting involved in an accident just because I wanted this guy off my bus.

I don't know why, but I turned my head to look at my passenger. I should have known better, or should I say I should have known what he was doing. Yep, sure enough, he was eating out of his handkerchief again. I watched as he took his forefinger and wiped it across his handkerchief as if his finger was a butter knife. I was waiting for the light to change to green and I was it wasn't happening fast enough for me. I watched him as he was finishing the swiping motion with the messy collection with boggers on his index finger. The man glanced up and looked my way. His eyes met mine. I didn't say word. I knew where those boggers were headed, his mouth.

Much to my surprise and delight, the man took the hanky with his left hand and wiped his right forefinger with it. The mess that was gathered on his finger was now gone. Man was I relieved. The traffic light change to green and I was rolling again. I could see the bus stop up ahead and I couldn't wait to get there. Again the chime sounded and I pulled the bus over to the curb by the bus-stop. The man got up from his seat and started to disembark the bus. As he passed by me he wished me a, "Good day." I acknowledged him and told him to watch his step getting off.   Every once in a while I think of the guy. I don't know what his story was, but; I hope things work out for him. Every once in a while when I getting ready to go to work and I'm reaching in my dresser drawer to grab a clean handkerchief, I think of that man.   It's amazing now, and scary, how when I look at a handkerchief, I think of how that man was using it as a lunchbox. I don't recall me ever eating boggers, but; I'm sure that that man gave me a reason not to start.

Made in the USA
San Bernardino, CA
19 December 2012